Differentiated Learning

*Language and literacy projects that address
diverse backgrounds and cultures*

Kathy Paterson

Pembroke Publishers Limited

KH

Acknowledgments

Many thanks to the students of the Teachers Education North, Grande Prairie Regional College, for their ideas.

Thanks also to William Shakespeare, the quintessential playwright and promoter of literacy, for his poignant phrases, a few of which I have added here and there.

Distributed in the U.S. by Stenhouse Publishers
477 Congress Street
Portland, ME 04101
www.stenhouse.com

We acknowledge the financial support of the Government of Canada through the Book Publishing Industry Development Program (BPIDP) for our publishing activities.
We acknowledge the Government of Ontario through the Ontario Media Development Corporation's Ontario Book Initiative.

Library and Archives Canada Cataloguing in Publication

Paterson, Kathleen M.
    Differentiated learning : language and literacy projects that address diverse classrooms / Kathy Paterson.

Includes index.
ISBN 1-55138-182-6

    1. Language arts (Elementary) 2. Individualized instruction. I. Title.

LC1200.P38 2005   372.6   C2004-907121-1

Editor: Kate Revington
Cover Design: John Zehethofer
Typesetting: Jay Tee Graphics Ltd.

Printed and bound in Canada
9 8 7 6 5 4 3 2

10/13/09

Contents

Afterword

Appendixes

Introduction: Differentiation Needn't Be Overwhelming

Though this be madness, yet there is method in't.

Then …

The teacher, her hands folded in front of her, calmly watched her class of sixteen students, ranging in ages from five to fifteen, prepare for the day. As the noise lessened, the older students automatically moved to assist the younger with whatever educational tasks had been assigned. The two nine-year-olds worked on a story they were eagerly composing about the recently completed harvest. Near the back, one girl was demonstrating to two others the best way to dip candles—a practical and authentic lesson for all three of them. One bright eleven-year-old was tackling problems from the single elementary math text in the one-room schoolhouse, while a less capable twelve-year-old watched eagerly, learning from his peer. The teacher knew that when the younger children were napping after lunch, she would have time to work with the older students on their projects. She watched her students in amazement. Such a motley crew they were, all unique, all independent. She was working with such an amazing range of ages and abilities. She loved her job! She smiled. It was going to be a great day!

Now …

The teacher, her hands overflowing with papers and files, watched anxiously as her twenty-nine students crowded into the room. It was going to be difficult to group these children for instruction today. The pre-Halloween materials in her arms wouldn't be suitable for the three children from the religious group that didn't celebrate Halloween; she'd need to find alternative work. Then she noticed that the two students who spoke English as a second language were cowering at the back of the room, unsure of what to do. One of them, newly emigrated from China, didn't speak a word of English. The other spoke Arabic with a few English words thrown in here and there. Nearby, the shy Métis student, who exhibited serious literacy deficits, already had her head down on her desk, trying to hide. Of course, the two gifted students were already at their desks: one, committed and conscientious, was already hard at work, while the other, continually bored and apathetic, was feigning sleep. In the hall the students from the nearby group home were trying to bully a peer into giving them his lunch, while a couple of the girls from "wealthier" homes were teasing the Hutterite girl about her outfit. The child from Ireland was trying to explain something to one of the Latino children, but his dialect was so strong that both students were getting frustrated.

A noise outside the door drew the teacher's attention to where her physically handicapped student's wheelchair was stuck and threatening to topple. As she rushed to help, she noted that her First Nations student was late—again. The teacher sighed. The curriculum materials in her arms felt heavy. She considered tossing them into the garbage and choosing a new plan for the day. What a motley crew she had before her, all unique, all needy. She was working with an amazing range of diversities. She loved her job, but it was going to be another really tough day!

The difference in the two anecdotes above is obvious. The teacher in the one-room schoolhouse faced students with a range of abilities, but she didn't have to deal with the cultural, intellectual, behavioral, linguistic, religious, physical, motivational, and socio-economic diversities of her modern-day counterpart. Although I must admit to playing devil's advocate in the second scenario, it is this teacher—the modern-day educator with a diverse range of students in the class—for whom this book is written.

Engaging All Students through the Project Approach

Oft expectation fails ...
especially when dealing with a diverse population.

Teachers are well aware that changing demographic realities have a significant impact on their classrooms. Today we live in a global society; in addition to mandated curriculum, our students need skills and knowledge to live harmoniously with other cultures. Educators, as well as having to deal with a rich mixture of student backgrounds, must also deal with the truism that not all students are alike. The catch phrase "no one size fits all" is significant. It reminds us to adjust the way we teach to meet the needs of the students, rather than expecting students to change to "fit" the curriculum. This is the premise of differentiated instruction: that instructional processes should vary in relation to diverse students in a classroom. Differentiated instruction, a process approach to teaching and learning, provides multiple student options with varying levels of complexity. The projects described in this book follow its tenets.

What every teacher wants to do is to help students become proficient communicators who are generally accepting of and empathetic to all people, regardless of race, color, or lifestyles. In other words, teachers want to create dynamic situations where language, literacy, and learning are promoted equally to and for all students. According to C. A. Tomlinson, content, process, and products are three elements of the curriculum that can be differentiated. With these in mind, the projects in this book manipulate *content* by aligning tasks, or projects, with inherent instructional goals and breaking down the objectives into manageable parts; manipulate *process* by making use of flexible groups; and manipulate *products* by encouraging students to take active part in creating projects for which there are varying expectations for results. In all situations, students are learning through communication—through language.

Halliday suggests that children learn language, learn about language, and learn through language. Schoolchildren develop particular ways of interacting and, thus, of learning language and learning about life—of developing both linguistic and socio-cultural knowledge. The approach suggested in this book capitalizes on this understanding by encouraging students to work with, and learn from, one another.

In general, today's classes consist of diverse groups of students, forming multicultural mosaics, wherein each student presents individual needs, potentials, and problems. Dealing with such a montage in the classroom has made the teacher's job increasingly difficult. As eager as educators are to celebrate diversity, teach according to the theory of differentiation, and treat all students with respect, continually adapting curriculum to meet the needs of all is almost impossible. I suggest that teachers begin with small steps. For example, using just one or two of the projects described in this book will facilitate differentiated instruction and authentic learning for all students.

Given that teachers must follow the curriculum while individualizing instruction to meet diverse students' needs—in other words, that they must teach differentially—I have designed a *project*-based approach to teaching that will help meet both demands. This approach is based on the understanding that *all* students, regardless of their backgrounds, cultures, or other diversities, learn best when motivated and involved, and that using the "arts" in a literacy program facilitates both of these basic requirements. Indeed, as teachers already know, when students are involved in meaningful projects, and are given enough time to develop them, reflect upon them, and receive feedback on them, motivation is high and learning becomes intrinsic. The approach offered in this book meets those requirements in a sensible, authentic, and easy-to-use curriculum-related manner. Basically, it involves teaching to a varied group of students by first establishing a project in which all of them, regardless of diversity, initially take part in the same manner, following which individuals branch off to work on a variety of different activities based on individual need and curriculum.

If the premise that *all* students can and will learn if involved and motivated in authentic, purposeful, and functional activities is accepted, then teachers need an ideas bank, or toolbox, that will facilitate meeting the needs of a diverse class population. This book is exactly that.

It is not my intent to suggest that teachers should teach exclusively using this type of approach; rather, these "lessons" can be used to supplement any curriculum, to enhance an appreciation of diversities, and to easily allow for individualized follow-up, or differentiation. It may be a good idea to use project-based learning once a week, or even once a month. Certainly, there are more projects within these pages than could be used in any given year. Teachers will choose the projects that interest them and their students and that best suit curriculum needs. At the very least, the ideas in this book will serve as a practical resource for busy teachers faced with extreme diversities in their classrooms, in other words, *all* teachers in our current schools.

I hope that the project approach offered in this book will help teachers to realize that diversity in a classroom, rather than being a problem, is an opportunity to enrich the learning of all students and that differentiated instruction is not as difficult as it may seem at first glance.

A Toolbox for Meeting Students' Diverse Needs

Be great in act as you have been in thought.

The *inquiry* approach to instruction allows students to first take part in an activity and then move to additional learning through seeking, questioning, researching, and experimenting. We, as adults, are well aware of the merits of this type of need-to-know learning. (*I need to know how to use this program to do my taxes. I need to know how to operate my complicated stereo equipment.*) By inviting students to become involved in an intrinsically motivating activity, one that has an obvious result, we are opening the door to inquiry learning.

The majority of the expected learning will come from the social constructivist nature of the projects and follow-up extensions. In other words, children learn best from one another. The interconnectedness of language, culture, involvement, peer support, and learning is incorporated into every project, making the diversities between students seem to disappear and, at the same time, reflecting the tenets of differentiated instruction.

The projects are designed to be low risk, easy to follow (even for students who do not speak the language), and highly motivating. They are simple for a teacher to demonstrate, the materials are inexpensive and readily available, and, in many cases, they naturally promote cultural awareness and respect. None of the projects, as far as I know, conflict with any ethnic, religious, or cultural beliefs, and many of them can be improved and expanded upon with the inclusion of information and language from more than the dominant culture.

Each project has curriculum connections and allows for considerable differentiation. Teachers will have their own ideas about how to follow up the original activities, but I have sought to provide a wealth of additional ideas and possible curriculum-based tasks that will readily adapt to the diversification of students as well as subjects and topics. A few "enhancement of learning" suggestions have been made for each project, simply as a basis from which teachers may work. Note that every project promotes the most common literacy activities, including journal writing, discussing, reflecting, and doing extended writing projects, such as stories and essays; however, these activities are not always listed.

Remember that, beyond the completion of the task itself, every project must have a *specific purpose*, based on both the needs of the students and the program of studies for a given jurisdiction. This is where the individual teacher's creativity comes together with the curriculum at each specific grade level.

The suggested projects are readily adaptable for all ages and, therefore, all grades from Kindergarten to Grade 9, requiring only minimal adaptations by teachers to meet the needs of different developmental groups. In some cases, suggestions for these adaptations have been included; in most cases, teachers themselves will see the necessary variations and quickly implement them. Where no special directions or adaptations appear, it is because I did not feel they were necessary.

Children should never be categorized according to stereotypical "groups"; however, for the sake of expediency only, I have delineated categories. I can thereby better suggest strategies that may prove beneficial for those particular students. In this book, I provide helpful suggestions for dealing with some of the most common student diversities requiring differentiated instruction. I offer hints for helping various students complete the projects, all the while knowing that children will constantly change their behaviors and consequent needs. The assumption is that most students, no matter what their culture, religion, abilities, or such, will be willing and able to take part in the projects.

Teachers may select a project by skimming the sections **What This Project Addresses** and **Project Overview** at the beginning of each selection. Making such a quick appraisal will allow you to select the project best suited for a particular purpose.

Please note that almost all of the projects require the gathering of some materials. Out-of-pocket costs should be minimal, though, and in cases where some cost may be incurred, teachers may approach principals for "class casual budgets" or even ask businesses for assistance. I am thinking particularly of disposable cameras for "Photo-Storybooks"—stores are usually willing to donate these when they are near or past the "best before" dates, and they still work fine.

In order to achieve the most authentic learning results, all projects should follow these criteria.

- The teacher knows for what ultimate purpose each project is carried out.
- The teacher draws on the students' own diverse, multicultural experiences to enhance every project, valuing and making use of their cultural and linguistic backgrounds.
- The teacher encourages discussion about the projects by constantly asking "Why?" and allowing students to speak in both the dominant language and in any other tongues present in the classroom.
- The teacher promotes collaborative activity even if the project begins with an individual focus.

Once a project has been selected, the following **Quick Check** serves as a general last-minute inspection to ensure that all is in order for subsequent success. Too often I have plunged into an activity fully believing I had been well prepared only to find I was missing some small, important detail. To help you avoid that, I offer brief, project-specific **Quick Checks**, which can be found right after **Steps for Teachers**.

Quick Check: All Activities

- Have I established a curriculum-based purpose for the project?
- Have I allowed for discussion, or "why?" time?
- Do I have a prepared "model" of the final project, that is, a picture or a sample?
- Have I all the necessary supplies on hand?
- Have I considered what kind of grouping may be necessary?
- If necessary, have I made arrangements for "support"—volunteers, language interpreters, older students, peers, and parents?
- Have I considered what "space"—clear desks, tables, floor—will be needed?
- Are the directions clear in my mind and made available in more than one modality, such as verbally and on a chart with visuals?
- Have I arranged for cleanup (are garbage bags on hand)?
- Have I designated enough time to complete the project in one sitting or will I need another time as well?

A Framework Based on Bloom's Taxonomy

Tomorrow, and tomorrow, and tomorrow …

The book has been organized according to Bloom's Taxonomy of Educational Objectives. This arrangement of levels of thinking, from the lower levels of Knowledge and Comprehension to the highest levels of Synthesis and Evaluation, provides a framework for teachers within which they can focus any intended learning. The separation of projects into categories based on this structure will allow teachers to select the ones that best fit the needs of their own students and circumstances. Although all the projects fit the criteria of most of these levels of critical thinking, I have separated them according to the thinking that predominates each task. However, depending on which curriculum connection activities teachers choose, the depth and range of skills change, making the groupings of projects according to levels somewhat hypothetical.

The categories used are the following:

- **Knowledge and Comprehension:** remembering previously learned material, translating and understanding

- **Application:** generalizing, using material and knowledge in new, innovative ways
- **Analysis:** breaking down of concepts, ideas, or informational materials in order to discover components
- **Synthesis:** composing, putting familiar material or knowledge together to form new wholes or arrangements or ideas

Since these categories increase in complexity from Knowledge to Synthesis, so do the accompanying projects. Those in the final chapter, Projects That Emphasize Synthesis, are, as a rule, the most involved and, by the same token, require the longest times to develop. It is not intended that the projects be carried out in a sequential manner, though; they may be used according to teacher or student interests and needs.

Evaluation, the final category in Bloom's Taxonomy, is important, but has not been treated as a separate section. That is because evaluation is inherent in every project, which involves an element of making informed judgments about the initial task and about any extension of learning activities that may take place.

It is important to remember that every project requires a curriculum-based purpose. The following table serves as a reminder for successful project planning.

Project Planning

1. Understand the purpose of the project and share that with students.
2. Share models, samples, or pictures of the completed project.
3. Model the steps for students, and accompany modelling and oral directions with written or illustrated directions.
4. Debrief the steps at least twice before letting students get started.
5. Have all materials ready before beginning the project, and allow time for cleanup.

Addressing Nine Kinds of Diversities

Be not afraid of greatness—or of diversity.

The following classifications and descriptors are intended to give teachers an idea of the diverse types of students who will benefit from the project-based ideas in this book. Please note that the descriptive categories are, at best, loose indicators of the particular needs of different children. At no time would I suggest *categorizing* students into any of these groups. Children are, first and foremost, children. Once that understanding is in place, we may consider that they present a vast array of differences in a classroom. Hence a child may reveal aspects of any number of the following diversities. The categories offered are intended to simplify the offering of possible teaching strategies.

Cultural Diversity

Students from different cultural backgrounds, including First Nations, Asian, Muslim, and Latino, as well as smaller cultural groups such as Hutterite and Mennonite, make up this large category. These children often come to school with a different view of education and learning than that of their dominant culture peers and teachers. They may appear less motivated to learn, to speak up in class, to work in groups, or to complete homework. Unfortunately, these behaviors are considered so much a part of "good student behavior" that many of these students get labelled "lazy" or "unmotivated." (Appendix A will help teachers understand aspects of cultural diversity.)

On the other hand, their cultural backgrounds may set them apart in exactly the opposite way; they may be less social or playful with peers, once again veering away from positive student behavior, as seen by the dominant culture.

It is common knowledge that children of diverse cultures come to school with a broad range of language and literacy experiences that are often quite different from those of European culture. Since these students may have difficulty understanding concepts outside their backgrounds, teachers become responsible for implementing culturally sensitive programs reflective of many cultural backgrounds. Not an easy task.

The project approach celebrates cultural diversity by allowing all students a chance to experiment with various projects, many of which are representative of cultures other than their own.

Linguistic Diversity

In the primary grades especially, we are seeing more and more students whose first language is not English. Keeping in mind that it often takes four to seven years for children to speak English proficiently, it is easy to understand why so many classes have these children as members. Just one non–English-speaking child in a class can pose a huge problem for already stretched-out teachers. In addition to the English as a Second Language (ESL) students, teachers may have students with different dialects; these too pose a teaching difficulty. And of course, cultural and linguistic diversities sometimes go hand in hand.

The following points are relevant when dealing with ESL students.

- Children develop language (first or second) through interactions with others.
- First or second language learning takes place only when learners have opportunity to use language in meaningful ways.
- No matter what ethnic background or what language they speak, children all use the same cognitive and linguistic processes to learn.
- Children who grow up in a mixed linguistic setting, for example, English and Aboriginal or French and English, may experience confusion in language use. Often fluency is not achieved in either language, or there is a strong, sometimes interfering dialect present in both tongues.
- Being in the presence of a strong role model—perhaps the teacher or a peer who speaks excellent, fluent English—is often the best way for a child to learn English.
- Daily involvement in activity that promotes language, in both the first language and the target language, facilitates literacy development, which leads to academic development.

Through the project approach, children who cannot speak the language, or who speak it poorly, take part in the project by watching the demonstrations of the teacher and the actions of peers. Also, the teacher may make minor adaptations for them, as suggested in the **Dealing with Diversities** section for each task.

Religious Diversity

The students in our schools come from all over the globe, so it is no wonder that many religious beliefs are reflected and some celebrations, such as the traditional Christmas or Halloween, at times discouraged. It is also true that many families have no religion at all, making religious-based celebrations foreign, and perhaps even uncomfortable, to these students. It is important for teachers to familiarize themselves with the boundaries of each student's beliefs, either by sending home an information-gathering letter early in the school year or by checking with the students themselves. (The Family Questionnaire beginning on the next page is a tool that you might use.)

The project approach is specifically designed so that students from all or no religious backgrounds can participate without the teacher having to prepare alternative activities for them.

Motivational Diversity

Lack of motivation, or apathy, is not a new diversity in the classroom, but its prevalence in modern schools needs to be addressed. Some students will be ready and eager to try anything and everything. Others will be indifferent no matter what the teacher suggests. Not to be confused with the student who exhibits symptoms of behavioral exceptionalities, the poorly motivated student often simply sits and chooses to do nothing. This student may be the last to whom the teacher gives attention, though, as the child seldom disturbs the class.

The project approach has a good chance of "hooking" most of the students most of the time, since all tasks provide students with authentic final projects.

Intellectual Diversity

Intellectual diversity is also not new in the classroom. In a Grade 4 class, for instance, there may be students reading from primer levels all the way to high school levels. As the curriculum expands (as it continually seems to do), so does the distance between the top and the bottom students in any classroom. In addition, with mainstreaming as the current educational practice, many students who in the past may have been segregated for instruction are now integrated into the "regular" classroom.

The project approach allows for this spread of abilities. All students begin with the same task, then split off into a variety of directions in the follow-up stage.

Physical Diversity

Today, physically, visually, and hearing challenged students may be integrated into regular classrooms. Sometimes, these students come with aides. More often than not, the aides are dealing with other charges elsewhere as well, and the regular classroom teacher is responsible for dealing effectively with students who represent physical diversity.

The project approach allows for peers to assist these children with the initial projects and for the teacher to diversify the follow-up activities to meet each child's needs. The challenged students are able to enjoy finished projects that are similar to their peers'.

Date _____

Dear Parent/Guardian,

Our classroom this year is a wonderful mixture of diverse personalities and backgrounds, and one of my goals is to celebrate that richness. To help me achieve that, please complete the following questionnaire, or as much of it as you want to, and return it to me as quickly as possible.

Throughout the year I will keep you informed of any special celebrations or activities I am planning, and, at times, I may ask for your input.

Your support and sharing would be most appreciated.

Sincerely,

Family Questionnaire

1. What is your ethnic or cultural background? _____

2. Do you celebrate any special days, seasons, or holidays that may be unfamiliar to many of the students in your child's class? Yes _____ No _____ If so, please provide the date(s) and a brief explanation. _____

3. If you answered "yes" to #2, would you be willing to visit our class and share information about these special days with us? Yes _____ No _____

4. Are there any special days, such as Christmas and Halloween, which your family does not celebrate? Yes _____ No _____ Which ones? _____ Would you rather your child not be involved in activities related to these times? Yes _____ No _____

5. Do you speak languages other than English in your home? Yes _____ No _____ If so, what language(s) and to what extent of the time? _____

6. It is important to celebrate and maintain first languages and languages other than the dominant one spoken in school. If you speak another language, would you be willing

   • to serve as an "as-needed" interpreter? Yes _____ No _____

   • to visit our class and share your language with us? Yes _____ No _____

7. Do you have any skills or interests, such as doing special crafts or storytelling, that you would be willing to share with the class? Yes _____ No _____

   Please describe briefly. _____

8. Are you able to help the class in any of the following ways?

   ❑ one-on-one tutoring (for example, reading with a student)

   ❑ special activities, such as parties and track and field days

   ❑ coaching

   ❑ extra-curricular activities, such as drama club

   ❑ escorting students on field trips

9. Does your family have any traditional heritage costume pieces or interesting items such as masks, toys, or any other artifacts that are representative of your culture or history? If so, what are they? _____

   Would you be willing to share them with the class? Yes _____ No _____

10. Is there anything else you would like me to know about your child or your family that may influence your child's success at school this year? Yes _____ No _____

    Please share. _____

Thank you for taking the time to complete this questionnaire. Feel free to contact me at _____ if you have any questions or concerns. Please leave a phone number or an e-mail address where you can be reached.

Socio-economic Diversity

Often there are wide gaps between the socio-economic backgrounds of the students in a given class. One student may come to school with every conceivable educational tool; another may be lucky to have a pencil. This gap creates a challenge for the teacher wanting to devise activities in which all students will take part with equality. It is important to avoid making the children from impoverished backgrounds feel inadequate or ill prepared to undertake projects, and bear in mind too that sometimes even the students we believe can "afford" supplies may not be able to.

The project approach starts all students off with the same "ingredients," or supplies, allowing for creativity and individuality from everyone.

Behavioral Diversity

The students who, for whatever reasons, "drive the teacher crazy" will always exist. For the teacher faced with myriad other diversities in a classroom, one acting-out student can seem like the proverbial last straw. More than simply apathetic, these students tend to be loud, distracting to others, and constantly seeking (if not demanding) the teacher's attention.

The project approach calls for intrinsically motivating, hands-on tasks that most children will find interesting. And we all know that managing those tough students means keeping them interested. A good practice is to invite students of this nature to help prepare and organize the activity. Give them extra responsibility for the success of the project.

Gifted Diversity

These students can excel in all academic tasks and for them the effective teacher supplies enrichment, acceleration, expansion of tasks, and more. They often require constant challenge so that they do not become bored and apathetic. As every teacher knows, if they don't get challenged, these brilliant students sometimes become underachievers and even behavioral problems.

The project approach opens many doors for these students to delve more deeply into concepts, to research areas of particular interest, and even to branch off completely on their own.

Quick Check: Teaching in a Diverse Population Classroom

The following checklist is provided as a reminder for all of us teaching in today's global village.

- Am I providing literacy experiences that reflect a variety of cultures?

- Am I providing literacy experiences that promote a variety of lifestyles and choices?

- Am I helping ESL students to value their first languages and keep fluent in them by encouraging dialogue in these languages?

- Do I keep foreign language dictionaries handy to help *all* students?

- Do I post environmental print, such as signs, directions, and names, in my classroom in several languages?

- Do I arrange to use bilingual tutors whenever possible?

- Do I encourage students to make and share videotapes in their first languages or tell about different cultural practices?

- Do I help share a student's first language and culture with the class by inviting adults, elders, or other knowledgeable persons to visit, make presentations, talk in their first languages, or just answer questions? (If the visitor speaks only in a foreign tongue, the students will have the experience of hearing another language and celebrating another form of communication.)

- Do I do research to learn about the various cultures in my class?

- Do I ask the librarian for up-to-date information and resources about a variety of cultures reflected in the classroom?

- Do I make it my practice to interview the families of children from other religions, cultures, and backgrounds (if possible) and "borrow" materials, pictures, artifacts, or any other relevant materials to share with the class in a discussion format?

- Do I actively try to find out about any cultural restrictions (e.g., not celebrating Halloween, Christmas, or Ramadan) and immediately plan for authentic, alternative activities, such as making thank-you cards instead of Christmas cards? (See Appendix B.)

- Through teamwork and consistent out-of-class involvement, do I encourage students to have a secure grasp on the first language before working on the second?

- Do I allow some work, such as letters home, to be done in the students' first language?

- Am I aware of possible discrepancies between the way classrooms operate and the ways in which students from different ethnic groups behave? (See Appendix A.)

- Do I provide directions in as many modalities as possible? (For example, talking about something and pointing to an illustrated chart.)

- Do I ensure that I avoid tokenism? (For example, not posting one poster of an Aboriginal on the wall as a way of accepting the First Nations culture? See Appendix C for positive ideas.)

1 Projects That Emphasize Knowledge and Comprehension

Knowledge and comprehension represent the lower level objectives in Bloom's Taxonomy, and are the areas most commonly addressed in many classrooms. They are specifically planned for by teachers to ensure that students not only have, and can recall, a knowledge base of facts, data, and concepts, but that they grasp the meaning of these. In other words, they can clarify and discuss what they have learned or are learning. Knowledge and Comprehension activities require students to recognize, recall, and interpret material, and address the ways and means of dealing with informational material.

Multiple choice and matching activities, as well as short answers and tasks requiring students to put things in their own words, are the most frequently used methods for testing these objectives. Questions beginning with *who, when, where, how,* and *what* reflect the Knowledge and Comprehension levels of thinking; however, as teachers are aware, these types of questions are likely used only as a beginning to further discussion and thinking.

Although the projects in this chapter may merge into the higher levels of thinking processes, they have been placed here due to their concentration on the skill clusters associated with knowledge and comprehension. The following represents the main skill clusters appearing in each of this chapter's projects.

Visit from an Elder: Every student observes, identifies, and describes the wonderful characteristics of an elder as well as paraphrasing, interpreting, and possibly documenting or recording information and wisdom shared by that special person.

People Puzzle Wall Mural: Students reproduce personal names by first selecting differentiated ways of doing this, then finally comparing approaches and discussing the "unified" nature of the completed puzzle.

Brain Teaser Scavenger: Students cluster, match, define, describe, and infer causes as they creatively identify as many items on a certain theme as possible.

Life Circle Wall Hangings: Students are required to define and outline their own lives. They will need to interpret, cluster, and document past happenings as well as make predictions for their futures.

Three Wishes: In this project, students discuss, recall, paraphrase, and summarize. Once they begin creating their own wishes, they will be carefully selecting and defining specific personal events so that they can set a realistic self-goal.

Noteworthy Names: Students take part in an in-depth observation and examination of their own names. They will initially discuss, paraphrase, interpret, and record information. When they put their individual books together, they will be defining and describing what they have learned about themselves.

Story Theatre Presentations: Students may be required to memorize but mostly to observe, paraphrase, interpret, and summarize in a low-risk drama-type situation.

Visit from an Elder

Friendship is constant in all other things.

What This Project Addresses

- cultural diversity
- the importance and value of elders, community seniors, and grandparents
- awareness of heritage
- listening and questioning
- respect for self and others
- manners and authentic introduction skills
- curriculum connections: Language Arts, Health, Social Studies

Project Overview

What a valuable resource our elders are. The value of using them in our classrooms has been well documented. This project involves each student in identifying an elder—a grandparent, other relative, or community senior—meeting with the elder, and inviting the elder to visit the classroom on a specified date to talk about something that interests both the students and the elder.

Most children have "an elder"; for those who do not, get in touch with community seniors at a local seniors' residence for willing candidates—there will be no shortage of them. I promise that if you make the effort to involve your class in this project, you will not be disappointed.

TINY TRUE TALE

Vicki: I didn't know your gran was so pretty. I really liked her dress. My gran wore pants when she came.
Dali: Sari. It's called a sari.
Vicki: Sari. Pretty name for a pretty dress.
Dali: (Smiling broadly) I have one too.
Vicki: You should wear it to school some day. I bet you'd look really pretty in it too.
Penny: My grandfather wore his special ceremonial necklace from his tribe when he came.
Dali: I guess all our elders are different. Like us.
Vicki: Yep! Come on, let's go find a swing before they're all taken.
The teacher smiled to herself. Until the day of her elder's visit, Dali had been alone—segregated from the other students most of the time. It appeared she was segregated no longer. Penny had seldom spoken at all. Now she was more than willing to talk about her grandfather, a Cree elder.

Materials

- large wall calendar to show dates of visits
- stationery for writing invitations
- thank-you notes and stamps
- Elder Questionnaire (see page 21)

Be sure to discuss the importance of elders: how their wisdom, stories, history, and accumulated knowledge are invaluable to all of us.

Steps for Teachers

1. Adapt the Elder Questionnaire as necessary for your grade and photocopy enough questionnaires to give one to each student. (See **Dealing with Developmental Levels** below.)
2. Make a large year calendar or list of months for marking upcoming visits. It's a good idea to limit visits to one per week, on a specific day at a specific time. This minimizes timetabling confusion.
3. Be sure to have stationery and thank-you cards ready.
4. Approach elders in the community to serve as surrogate seniors for any students without a personal elder in their lives.
5. Discuss "elders" with the class. You could bring up the different ways elders are treated in different cultures, and ask for input from any non-dominant culture students. Discuss all the ways elders can contribute to the class (e.g., special talents, memories of historical events, stories, poetry, and favorite readings).
6. Have students think of elders they would like to invite to class and why.
7. Role-play inviting elders, dealing with the questionnaires, and introducing the elders to the class.
8. Discuss the concept of a sharing circle, where all members may talk and ask the elder questions after the elder has finished telling or presenting.
9. Inform the principal of your intentions and provide the dates of scheduled visits.

Quick Check: Visit from an Elder

- Have I informed the principal of my plans?
- Do I have enough "spare" seniors available to visit?
- Have I determined how to arrange my class into a circle for the visits?

Steps for Students

1. Students think of an elder they would like to invite to class. If they cannot think of one, they consult the teacher.
2. Working with classmates, they practise making invitations to elders.
3. Students write invitations, telling what day and time they would like the elders to visit based on the teacher's predetermined dates and times. The letters should suggest a number of possible visitation times from which to choose.
4. Each student calls or visits the elder with a questionnaire after the invitation has been accepted.
5. Using the information from the questionnaire, the student plans a good introduction for the elder, and contacts the elder again to confirm the date and time of the visit.
6. When the elder comes to school, the student makes proper introductions not only to the class, but also to the principal and secretary. Even primary students can handle this as long as they have had time to practise making the specific introduction beforehand. This provides an excellent learning experience for them.
7. After an elder's visit, the student writes a thank-you card and mails it.

Dealing with Diversities

Cultural: This is such a wonderful way to invite elders from different cultures that I suggest *all* students invite their elders to talk, at least in part, about their cultural backgrounds.

Linguistic: If an interpreter is necessary, try to provide one so that the elder can speak to the class in his or her first language. Students need to be exposed to other languages. If the elder speaks limited English, encourage the students to learn some words from the elder. Make it a mutual learning experience.

Religious: Encourage these students, either those belonging to any non-dominant religions *or* students from Christian or atheist homes if they so choose, to bring a strong advocate for their faith to class as a learning experience for all.

Socio-economic: Sometimes, these children feel embarrassed about bringing a relative. If hesitancy occurs, discuss in private with the student. Perhaps arrange for an elder from the local community to come instead or offer whatever assistance is needed to create a comfortable experience. (On one occasion, I picked the grandparent up on my way to school as he didn't have cab fare.)

Behavioral: If any of these students refuse to invite someone they know, suggest a community elder to them, and make the necessary arrangements for the two to meet. Seniors are usually very willing to cooperate. If possible, try to connect a child with an elder who had similar tastes as a youth (e.g., young ball player with a senior citizen who played ball).

Dealing with Developmental Levels

Kindergarten to Grade 3: Simplify the questionnaire. Practise good "sharing circle" manners and listening skills. Use templates for thank-you cards if necessary.

Grades 4 to 9: Encourage higher level questioning. Practise asking *good* questions of each other so as to avoid the familiar *How old are you?* or *Is that your real hair color?*

Making Curriculum Connections and More

Language Arts: Students may write reflections after the visit of an elder. They may create comparison charts and graphic organizers, perhaps looking at two elders of quite different backgrounds and pointing out what may be a surprising number of similarities. Other activities include collecting and recording data from interviews and questionnaires, and brainstorming ways of showing respect, such as offering a helping hand and listening attentively.

Health and Social Studies: Students may draw conclusions about similarities between different peoples. They may write about or discuss feelings of pride in cultural backgrounds or discuss stereotyping, cultures, immigrating and emigrating, and the wealth of diverse populations. Elder visits may provide an opportunity to understand history, as told by the elders. Students may also explore ways of demonstrating respect for members of the community through appropriate discussions, letters, interviews, and more.

Elder Questionnaire

1. What would you like to talk to our class about? (Please see the list of possible topics below. You do not have to choose one of these; they are suggestions only.)

   _____

2. Do you have any objects, supplies, or pictures you would like to share with the class?
   Yes _____ No _____ If so, what?

   _____

3. Do you have a way to get to our school? Yes _____ No _____

   _____

4. Would you like to share anything about how or when you came to Canada?
   Yes _____ No _____ If so, what? How long have you lived in Canada?

   _____

5. What name would you like to be introduced by? _____

   _____

6. Is there anything you would like me to tell the class before you visit us?

   _____

   _____

Possible Topics

- Events from your early life (at school, in the community, on a farm)
- Stories you would like to tell
- Stories about your cultural background
- What it was like when you were a child
- How the value of money has changed
- What expectations were put on you in your youth

People Puzzle Wall Mural

When shall we three meet again ...

What This Project Addresses

- class cohesion
- the importance of all individuals in the class
- individual differences and similarities
- the importance of names
- pride in belonging
- curriculum connections: Language Arts, Health, Social Studies, Mathematics, Physical Education, Science

Project Overview

All teachers know the knot in the stomach when a student's name escapes them—even if it is only the first week of school. Students *expect* us to know their names. What's more, they truly *need* to be recognized by their names. That's how important our names are to us! They are a vital part of what makes each of us an individual. This project puts everyone's name in the limelight (and gives the teacher faced with a new class a chance to connect names to faces).

In addition to knowing names, it's always a good idea to represent every student in the class in some highly visual manner, on your classroom walls. The completed project, in this case, is a compilation of puzzle pieces joined to make a *connected* representation of your class. It can be as simple or as complicated, as small or as large, as you want. It can be a puzzle for putting together in a learning centre or an interesting wall mural. In any event, students of all ages are amazed at its apparent complexity and will spend many minutes just gazing at it. Because every student's name is involved, the project becomes important to them.

Basically, students print, write, or draw their names on pieces of an interconnecting puzzle; the pieces are then put together. Simple! Effective! (See Figure 3.)

TINY TRUE TALE

"I don't think I should use my real name," Manpreet whispered to the teacher after she had explained the People Puzzle to the children.

"Why?" the teacher whispered back.

"Because it's not like the other kids' names and they might not like it."

"Your name is so cool," piped up a neighbor who, happily in this case, had been nosy. "And besides, it's everyone's name. And you are in this class just like me."

The teacher smiled and thought "out of the mouths of babes ... "

Manpreet's name, through sheer luck, ended up right in the middle of the finished mural. He seemed extremely pleased. And not one student had anything but positive things to say about their People Puzzle.

Materials

- two sheets of same-size heavy-weight paper
- scissors

- white glue
- coloring mediums—crayons, pencil crayons, felt markers, oil pastels

Discuss the wonderful variety of names in the class. After you give your full name, ask each student to share his or her complete name. Acknowledge and celebrate all names by pointing out something interesting, unusual, or beautiful about each. Express an interest in knowing more about the names, and share what you know about your own name. For example: *I know that Kathleen means "pure." I don't know if I'm pure or not, but my parents thought …*

Steps for Teachers

1. Divide poster paper in quarters, then roughly divide each section into the number of pieces that equal one-quarter of the students in your class (see Figure 1).
2. Draw "puzzle" type shapes in each quarter, to equal the number of sections. You can use the typical curved shapes (see Figure 2) or more rigid, straight-edged shapes. The choice is up to you. Just remember that you have to cut these shapes out and then reassemble them.
3. Before cutting the shapes out, be sure to number each shape in sequence (see Figure 3). The numbers not only serve to show directionality to students (top/bottom, left/right), they also help in reassembling the puzzle. Use a pencil because it can be erased by students after they have written their names.
4. Cut the pieces out. (See Figure 4.)
5. Once students have prepared all pieces and you have them in hand, return the pieces to their original places and glue on the second card. You need to wait until you have them all together because sometimes some pieces "grow" in the decorating process. Or, if you want to make the puzzle available for younger students to use in a learning centre, do not return pieces to the second board; instead, glue them to a heavy backing one piece at a time.

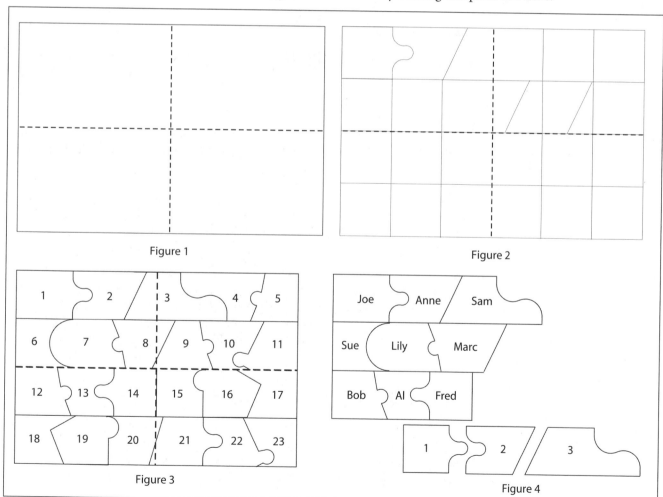

Figure 1

Figure 2

Figure 3

Figure 4

6. Make a sign to place near the completed People Puzzle, as follows:

> **This Is a People Puzzle, Each Person's Piece a Token.**
> **If Just One Piece Is Missing, The Puzzle Will Be Broken.**

Quick Check: People Puzzle Wall Mural

- Does each student have a puzzle piece in the correct direction, that is, top/bottom, right/left?
- Do students with longer names have big enough pieces?

Steps for Students

1. Students write their names in any creative way they want, using the numbers to guide them where to start.
2. They rewrite the numbers that were on their pieces *very small* in the top left-hand corner of the piece, in pencil. If they want to, they may erase the original large pencil numbers.
3. Students make their puzzle pieces colorful and personal. When ready, they return their pieces to the teacher.

Dealing with Diversities

Cultural: As shown in **Tiny True Tale**, some children may be hesitant to write given names, especially if they feel their names are "different. "People Puzzle" is a wonderful opportunity to celebrate the many beautiful, different names in your class *before* beginning the project.

Linguistic: Encourage the writing of names in students' first languages. Some other students may want to get help from the ESL students to write their names in another language too. Encourage this as a way of celebrating languages.

Motivational and Behavioral: Asking these students to assist you in cutting out the individual pieces ahead of time, and then helping you to reassemble them, may be enough to ensure their cooperation.

Gifted: Challenge these students to find the most unusual names in history and share their findings with the class, or to find out the historical backgrounds to their own family names. Rather than making this an addition to the basic project, offer them the opportunity to do this *instead of* some activity in which they do not need the extra work. A page of review material might be an example. This approach will hold true for any extension-of-project activities with which you challenge these students.

Dealing with Developmental Levels

Kindergarten to Grade 3: With very young children, lightly print their names on the pieces and allow them to copy or write over your printing. This prevents upside down or backwards names on the completed project. Of course, students who cannot print yet should be encouraged to draw instead.

Grades 4 to 9: Once students realize what's going on, some may want to write their names so that they will end up upside down or backwards. Let them go for it. It makes the final product more interesting. Encourage all manner of creativity.

Making Curriculum Connections and More

Language Arts: Students may write poetry about the finished People Puzzle—it works especially well to have them write formula poems, such as acrostics and cinquain. Students could write class stories, where every student is a character. Alternatively, they could debate the many pros and cons of working together as a whole class or several members of the class who do not know one another well could engage in dialogue journalling. Another idea is to list and categorize everything that the class does together that is improved by shared effort and cooperation.

Health: The class could discuss what makes a community "stick together" or how we are all alike and yet all different. Students could also list needs that can be better met by large groups working as one than by individuals.

Science: Related concepts include studying atoms and molecules (parts of wholes).

Mathematics: Learning about parts, wholes, fractions, multiplication, and division relates to the theme.

Physical Education: Students could play cooperative games, take part in team sports, or discuss the importance of team spirit and fair play.

Here is a great adaptation on the People Puzzle theme that you might not have thought of. It works very well in the classroom.

Make a Human Snake: Create a long, curvy snake-like figure (see Figure 5). This can be any size you want it to be, but bigger is better. Divide the "snake" into as many parts as you need—one per student—and number the pieces in sequence. Allow students to decorate the pieces with their names and more. Put the snake back together and mount on your wall. You'll have an excellent, very personal wall mural!

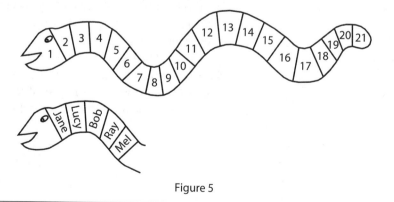

Figure 5

Brain Teaser Scavenger

How poor are they that have not patience.

What This Project Addresses

- critical thinking skills
- clarification of ideas
- communication skills
- cooperation and group-work skills
- curriculum connection: Language Arts

Project Overview

There is a saying that children come to school as question marks and leave as periods. How awful! How true! What is also true is that we generally make use of only a tiny part of our brains; however, with effort we can enhance brain functioning, just as with exercise we can enhance muscle functioning. Surely part of our roles as educators, then, is to help our students exercise their brains. "Brain Teaser Scavenger," in which students produce innovative word walls, does just that.

Although "Brain Teaser Scavenger" does not involve the creation of an object, it is a valuable project, especially in a classroom with a diverse population. It involves critical thinking and collective effort in a low-risk, fun-filled, game-like pursuit. The idea is for groups to *compete* (or not, depending on the teacher's purpose) to come up with the most words or ideas that fit into categories predetermined by the teacher. The project is an offshoot of the well-known scavenger hunt, but is done *in* the classroom, at desks or tables where each group, provided with a "list" (see examples on page 29) and some writing paper, searches their brains for the items required.

It is important that the groups are heterogeneous, so that students with any types of diversities will feel completely involved. The teacher points out that "all ideas count, no matter what language they're expressed in."

The task can be subject to a time limit of fifteen minutes, or it can be an ongoing pursuit, with group members adding ideas for a period of one week. The latter method allows for students to get help from home; ESL students then have the opportunity to "bring" words or ideas in their first language, which celebrates the variety of languages in the class.

The final task of the groups that "win"—in other words, that have the most or best selection of words or ideas—is to transfer their full lists onto large chart paper for sharing with the rest of the class. The most "effective" or "complete" lists can then be mounted on walls; these make interesting resources for everyone.

"I always hated scavenger hunts, until we did this one," Allie said as she stared with complete fascination at her group's chart on the wall. "This one was fun. And my grandmother had lots of ideas for it too."

"Yeh, but my group had more words than yours," sulked Robert. "Ours should have been on the wall."

"But did your group have all the French words?" Allie said smugly.

"Do you even know what those words mean?" Robert asked, unwilling to be deterred by this seemingly unquestionable fact.

"I do now," Allie replied with a smile.

Materials

- lists for brain "scavenging"—see "A Variety of Lists for Brain Teaser Scavenger," page 29.
- paper and pencils
- large chart paper and felt pens

Steps for Teachers

To begin, draw a chalk dot, about 1 cm in diameter, on the board. Ask the students what it is. At first, students may simply respond "a dot" or "a mark." Try to draw out as many unusual responses as possible, such as "ladybug, end of an eraser, drop of honey, pimple." (The younger the students, the more creative they tend to be.) Lead the discussion to the idea of novelty, originality, and creativity of thought, in preparation for the inquiry type of thinking necessary for the scavenger hunts.

1. Create lists according to what you want your students thinking or talking about. It is easy to do this for any subject content area.
2. Determine heterogeneous small groups.
3. If desired, come up with little "prizes" since the activity can have a game format.

Quick Check: Brain Teaser Scavenger

- Have I arranged the groups so that they are as "equal" as possible?
- Have I made the necessary arrangements for ESL students?

Steps for Students

1. Each group decides who in the group will be the "writer," the person who quickly records all the ideas.
2. Students talk about the "topics" and brainstorm for as many ideas as possible. If given a time limit, students work quickly; if they have a longer time, they may take the ideas home and invite friends and family to add their ideas too.
3. Each group that "wins" a category transfers ideas neatly to chart paper.

Dealing with Diversities

Cultural and Linguistic: Once these students understand what is expected, encourage use of ideas from their cultures or expressed in languages other than the dominant class language. For ESL students, it may be a good idea to explain the task to them beforehand, using visuals and interpreters so that they do not feel frustrated when peers quickly give words and ideas.

Physical: Often children who are confined to wheelchairs, for example, are amazing thinkers. Perhaps this is because they spend more of their energy thinking than doing. Frequently, they make good group leaders, and others readily accept them in these roles, particularly for this activity.

Gifted: These students also make good group leaders for this project. In addition, challenge them to research the brain and share their findings with the class. There are many wonderful sites for brain study on the Internet, and students will surely find them fascinating.

Dealing with Developmental Levels

Kindergarten to Grade 3: Keep the challenges easy and fairly basic for these students. For Grade 1, arranging for an older student or volunteer to "scribe" will speed up the thinking process as they will not have to take time to print unfamiliar words.

Grades 4 to 9: This is a great activity for cross-curriculum incorporation. Simply make the headings fit the curricular area.

Making Curriculum Connections and More

Language Arts: Students may write about one or several of the new, interesting words or ideas listed on the mounted word wall or wall chart.

Multi-lingual Crossword Puzzles: Here is another brain teaser to introduce your students to. The directions are simple. Divide students into groups so that each group has at least one child who speaks a language other than the dominant one. Provide each group with a large squared grid (from a math graphing unit). Each group's task is to find words in at least two languages that have the same meaning and that can intersect as in a crossword puzzle. See Appendix D for a photocopiable example.

	C			**English (horizontal)**
	H			**French (vertical)**
C	A	T		
	T			

If students can get several words to intersect, so much the better. And what a wonderful way to stimulate brains *and* celebrate linguistic diversity within your classroom!

Note: An excellent Web site for additional "brain teasers" by grades is http://www.eduplace.com/math/brain/index.html.

A Variety of Lists for Brain Teaser Scavenger

LIST 1 Over/Under: Language Skills

Think of as many things as possible that are

- under your bed – over your bed
- under the ocean waves – over the rainbow
- under the ground – over the treetops
- under your shoe – over your head
- under a rock – over a beach

LIST 2 Ways to Say: Literacy and Health

Think of as many ways as possible to say or show each of the following:

- Thank you. Please.
- I appreciate that.
- I'm sorry.
- Can I help you?
- Hello. Good-bye.

LIST 3 What's True?: Science

Think of as many words that are related to each of the following topics as you can:

- Weather
- The universe
- Wetlands
- Electricity
- Colors

LIST 4 Ways to Use: Language Skills

Think of as many ways as you can to use each of these items:

- Scissors
- Ruler
- Apple
- Paper clip
- Coat hanger

LIST 5 Things That Can: Language Skills

Think of as many examples of things that can

- be opened
- be mended with tape
- be weighed without scales
- fly
- float

LIST 6 Things That Can't: Science Skills

Think of as many things as possible that can't

- be mended (e.g., burst balloon)
- be photographed (e.g., wind)
- be gift wrapped (e.g., warm wishes)
- be changed (e.g., the spinning of the earth on its axis)
- be found once lost (e.g., breath)

Life Circle Wall Hangings

I go, and it is done; the bell invites me.

What This Project Addresses

- the cyclic nature of every living thing
- an awareness and comprehension of self
- creativity and persistence
- communication through representation
- goal setting
- curriculum connections: Language Arts, Health, Science, Art

Project Overview

Every teacher appreciates the importance of helping students to develop self-awareness, self-respect, and self-confidence. Sometimes, however, it is difficult to encourage them to look closely at themselves and to examine their existence in the world. Children are egocentric. They live in the here and now. How can we help them to understand something as abstract as the cyclic nature of existence?

This project helps them to do this by inviting them to break their lives into four or more *chunks* (students like this term and can understand it, so I will refer to the quadrants as chunks from now on); students also illustrate or write about each chunk. The chunks are as follows: (1) Infant (preschool), (2) Student (including the rest of the school years), (3) Adult, and (4) Senior (old age). Each chunk will be identified by the year-span: for example, 1996–2002 might cover the preschool years. The final chunk, from the date at which they believe their old age will begin, will end in a "?" indicating the uncertainty about time of death.

Since most young people don't ever imagine themselves getting "old," this project encourages them to gain insights into the whole aging process; it also helps them think about their futures as well as develop more appreciation for elders. Students are called to identify at least one situation, personal quality, or idea associated with each chunk of their lives. Doing this will require making predictions and wishes for the future. Because their predictions must be based on reality (as much as possible), students, in essence, will be making long-term goals. "Living on Mars," for example, would not be an appropriate representation for the third chunk.

Each student is given two circles on heavy paper. Construction paper or heavy copy paper will work, but slightly heavier is even better. One circle will be about 5 cm in diameter smaller than the other. The smaller circle will have a portion marked to cut out a "window" (see Figure 6). This circle is simply a "mask," whose purpose is to cover the entire underlying circle and reveal only what can be seen through the "window."

The bigger circle is where the action is. Divided into fourths, this circle is clearly marked around the edge with the appropriate "time frames" (see Figure 7) and the section of circle beneath the time frame is decorated in some way to illustrate that time period, or "chunk," of the student's life. Students may draw, write text, or decorate using collage. Some students may wish to make each chunk completely different. For example, a student might prepare a *drawing* of a baby; show *pictures* of books and school materials, as well as *text* about school; make a *collage* including a magazine picture of a man in a business suit and other images related to being a lawyer; and include a *photograph* of a grandfather reading to a small child, with a few words of a student-written *poem* about grandfathers.

The two cardboard circles are joined with *brads* so that the inner circle can be turned. Although this project *sounds* complicated, it is really quite easy and the results are exciting. Students love to turn the inner wheels of peers and thus learn more about others and their hopes and dreams.

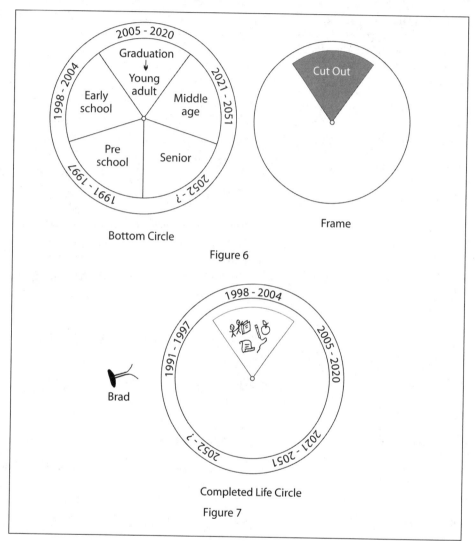

Bottom Circle

Frame

Figure 6

Completed Life Circle

Figure 7

TINY TRUE TALE

"Are you going to make a Life Circle, Ms X?" asked a small voice eagerly.

"No," answered Ms X.

"Why not?"

Before Ms X could reply, another small voice answered innocently and sweetly, "Because she's so old she'd have to put a grave in her last chunk and who'd want to see that? Isn't that right, Ms X?"

Brads come in various shapes and sizes and are available in craft stores or in some stationery or office supply stores in boxes of 20 or 30.

Be sure to engage the whole class in a discussion about Life Circles— pasts, presents, and futures—and about making appropriate goals (or wishes) for the future. Relate the Medicine Wheel, an important facet of Aboriginal culture, to the students and their lives. Be sure to point out how a circle has no beginning and no end. Discuss other things that happen in cycles, such as the life of a frog or butterfly. Discuss what has happened so far in the students' lives; then ask them to make predictions about their futures.

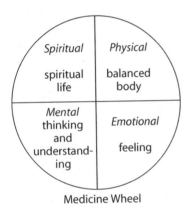

Medicine Wheel

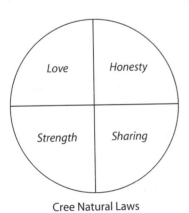

Cree Natural Laws

Figure 8

Materials

- two card circles for each child
- one "brad" (a small device with a head and two arms that permits turning) per student
- magazines, scissors, and glue
- clips for the centres of the circles
- coloring materials
- white paper (for drawing and gluing to circles)
- pictures or overheads of the Medicine Wheel of the First Nations people (see Figure 8)

Steps for Teachers

1. Prepare the cardboard circles as described above.
2. Locate any information you wish to share about the Aboriginal Medicine Wheel and Circle of Life, as well as details about other obvious circles of life, such as that of a familiar plant or animal.
3. Introduce the project to the whole class and then have students break into groups.
4. Provide specific questions to discuss in groups, such as *What sorts of things have been important to you up till now? What might be important for the rest of your school lives? What will you be like as adults?*
5. Have small-group discussions about making adult goals and being elders, before letting students decorate these two chunks, as they will need time to think and talk about these areas of their lives.

Quick Check: Life Circle Wall Hangings

- Do I have a sample wheel to use as a model, even if the chunks are not decorated?
- Do students have an adequate understanding of what's involved in making future goals?

Steps for Students

1. Students cut out their circles and the windows on the smaller circles.
2. They label the time frames on the bigger circle, in the part marked for them. They then divide their bottom circles into four or more parts. Each part will be directly related to the dates that tell about it.
3. Students decide on one or more important events for their *preschool* and *now* chunks. They decorate both of these chunks in any way they want, keeping the decorations in the right parts of the circle. They may decorate directly on the bottom circle or decorate on a piece of white paper which is cut out and glued to the circle.
4. Students then think about their futures. In small groups, they discuss future plans and goals and give one another ideas about how to represent different futures.
5. Next, students talk about any seniors they know. What are some things they really like about them? Students choose something they like about elders and imagine themselves as elders with those characteristics. They consider such questions as whether they would want to have grandchildren or to be travelling.

6. Students decorate the last two chunks of their lives.
7. Finally, each of them fastens the two circles together so that the inside one turns and shows different life chunks, one chunk at a time. They include their names somewhere on the frame circles.

Dealing with Diversities

Cultural: Encourage these students to include any ideas related to their specific cultures. At the very least, a child born in another country could add the name of that country in the first chunk.

Linguistic: Encourage these students to use text in both their first language and English in the different chunks of their wheels.

Religious: Encourage these students to include facts relating to their religious beliefs in their chunks; these are an important part of their lives and this is an excellent place to include them in a school project.

Physical: Because this project involves working in fairly small spaces, it may be necessary to arrange for individual help for these students.

Gifted: Encourage these students to include more abstract illustrations and text in their chunks or to break their pages into more chunks (and change the window size accordingly). Empower them to "think metaphorically" by providing them with some samples, for example, *I will find my pot of gold by …*

Dealing with Developmental Levels

Kindergarten to Grade 3: As noted previously, it may be necessary to have the circles and windows already cut out for younger students. In addition, stiffer circles of Bristol board are easier for them to use and if the bottom circle is white or beige colored, they will be able to work directly on that circle and bypass the cutting and gluing of additional paper.

Grades 4 to 9: The older and more capable the students are, the more chunks they can break their lives into. For instance, some students enjoy adding chunks for teen years, early adulthood, middle age, and so on.

Making Curriculum Connections and More

Language Arts: Activities include writing autobiographies, summaries of stories or expository text, and dialogues based on imagining what people were saying in a specific chunk.

Health: Students could discuss the importance of personal goals as well as the importance and value of elders in the community.

Social Studies: Here is a good opportunity to learn about the First Nations people, especially the Medicine Wheel, the Circle of Life, and sharing circles.

Science: The class could take an opportunity to learn about the life cycles of all living things in a specific ecosystem or to research topics such as metamorphosis and compost.

Art: Students could explore a variety of ways to illustrate a point visually.

Three Wishes

We are such stuff as dreams are made of.

What This Project Addresses

- appreciation, respect, and tolerance for needs of others
- comprehension of literature
- sensitivity and empathy
- personal goal setting
- knowledge-based predictions
- support of ideas with relevant facts
- curriculum connections: Language Arts, Health, Social Studies

Project Overview

I wish I may, I wish I might, make this wish come true tonight! I wonder how many of us have said that at least once in our lives? A safe guess would be almost all of us. Perhaps the message here is that all people of all ages like to make wishes. Most certainly our students enjoy anything to do with wish making. Their appreciation for the many Disney videos on the market pays witness to this fact. "Three Wishes" capitalizes on children's intrinsic enjoyment of making wishes, but takes it a step further in that they are invited to make wishes for *others* as well as themselves.

Beginning with the telling or reading of the short story "The Three Wishes," students are encouraged to discuss the difference between personal and unselfish wishes. Then they are invited to discuss wishes they might make for larger communities, such as "our town/city," "the people of ___" and, eventually, for "our school."

In small groups, students brainstorm all the positive wishes they would make for their school, if money was no object. Remind them that their wishes should pertain to the physical school itself, *not* to specific staff members.

Each group then agrees upon and transfers their two *best* wishes onto the strips of colored paper. All the strips are glued in collage technique (see Figure 9) to a large piece of paper for wall mounting. This example of combined effort makes an interesting discussion piece and also serves as a gentle hint to the powers that be of possible future directions the school might take.

The project is taken further when students make a wish for someone else and one for themselves. The wishes must be realistic (obtainable in theory at least), and the self-wish must relate to a future goal (*I wish I would get an 80 percent in the math test because I want to be an engineer when I grow up and I'll need to be able to do math*). Self-wishes should also relate to something over which students have some control, for example, *I wish my mark in Language Arts was higher.*

Wishes for *others* are put in envelopes and given to the person for whom the wish is written. To ensure that everyone gets a wish, you may choose to draw names in the class and have students write a wish for the person whose name was drawn.

Self-wishes are folded and put in a large envelope. At the end of the year, you may revisit these self-wishes and discuss in small groups (or individually with students) what steps have been taken to reach the goals or make the wishes come true.

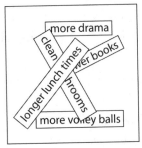

Figure 9

Patrick was just about the loudest, most restless child ever! When he wrote his second wish, it was for his mom. It read, "I wish my mom wouldn't get so mad at me when I can't sit still and do my homework. I feel scratchy and just can't sit. I wish she wouldn't feel so bad at me because it gives her a headache so I guess I give her a headache."

Although it wasn't a typical wish for someone else, the teacher allowed him to take it home anyway, thinking some good might come from it. Patrick's wish for himself was, "I wish I could sit still. I hate it when I am so noisy and can't sit still and get my work done."

This time the teacher felt it was necessary to talk to the parents about the wishes. After getting permission from Patrick to share this wish with his parents, she had them in for a conference. The end result was that Patrick was taken to a doctor, put on a special diet and some short-term medication—and both of his wishes came true. The parents said they just didn't know he was having trouble. He was their only child and they thought all little boys were like that. So, the moral of the story is, sometimes teachers can help make wishes come true.

Materials

- the story "The Three Wishes" (see pages 37 and 38)
- long strips of paper, about 15 cm wide and 60 cm long, for School Wishes
- smaller strips from 8 by 11 paper cut into about four strips horizontally for second and third wishes
- envelopes for second wishes
- a large envelope for all third wishes

Steps for Teachers

As a way to introduce this project, you might quote, "I wish I may, I wish I might … " to the students and open a class discussion about making wishes. Ask if anyone has ever made a wish for someone else or made a wish that has come true.

1. Photocopy the story "The Three Wishes" and engage the class in discussions as indicated in **Project Overview**.
2. Break students into groups and have them work together to make their School Wishes. Encourage them to be specific when making a wish and to back the wish up with logical reasons and information. Some wish ideas might be as follows:
   a. Better playground—more swings because the kids fight over them and the big kids always get them
   b. More volleyballs—because we have to share and it would be better if we each had one to practise with
   c. Another custodian—because the bathrooms are not very clean and it's too big a school for the caretaker to take care of all alone
   d. Longer lunch break—because if we want to go home we can't and it gets too crowded in the lunchroom. (We could stay later in the afternoon to make up the difference.)
3. Have students make their second and third wishes.
4. Remember to follow up with the third wish at a later date.
5. Glue the School Wishes onto a large piece of paper (or invite a couple of students to do this for you).

Quick Check: Three Wishes

- Do the students understand the importance of making *specific* wishes for others and themselves? (You may need a mini-lesson on specificity.)
- Are there any students who may need individual help to think about their personal wishes?

Steps for Students

1. Students in small groups talk about all the things that might make their school a better place. They choose the two best School Wishes and print them neatly on the paper provided.
2. On their own, each student writes a wish for someone else, ensuring that the wish is not silly, can probably be obtained, will make that person happy, and will be important to that person.
3. Finally, students write wishes for themselves, ensuring that their wishes are not silly, can probably be obtained or at least worked toward, relate to their futures, and are realistic.

Dealing with Diversities

Linguistic: Due to the largely linguistic nature of this project, it will be necessary to arrange for these students to hear the story in their first language if possible, and have the directions explained in that language as well. Students may write their wishes in whichever language they want to. It may be a good idea to ask any students with capabilities in another language to translate School Wishes, writing directly under or over the English versions on the strips of paper.

Religious: As far as I know, no religion disapproves of the making of wishes for others, but if a child seems reticent, check this out before insisting that the student proceeds.

Motivational: These children may require additional motivation to carry out this task. Inviting them to put together the final School Wishes chart for you might work.

Gifted: Challenge these students to write their own stories based on wishes that did or did not come true. Encourage them to include a moral in their stories.

Making Curriculum Connections and More

Language Arts: Extensions include writing reflections on the story "The Three Wishes," discussing or writing about the idea that when we make a wish for someone else, it makes us feel good too, writing short letters to accompany the wishes for friends or relatives, and writing business letters to the principal, school board, or even Minister of Education to express some of the ideas discovered during the School Wishes section of this project.

Health: The activity could lead into discussions about basic needs in addition to the needs for love, acceptance, appreciation, and more. Students could also discuss or write journal entries on "what sorts of things make me feel good about myself?" (self-awareness)

Social Studies: Students may learn how communities meet needs and have met needs throughout history.

The Three Wishes

There was once a young man in a faraway land, who, while walking in the woods near his home, came upon a curious, blue-green bottle hidden inside a hollow tree stump. It was strange how he had come upon that particular tree stump in that particular part of the woods, for he didn't usually walk there. As he held the beautiful bottle in his hands, it caught the rays of the sun and seemed to sparkle with some inner magic.

"It must be a wishing bottle," the young man thought, for most certainly he had heard of such a thing. "I will make a wish."

Before he could do anything more, he heard a beautiful voice speaking clearly. It seemed to come from the bottle. "You have three wishes. You cannot wish for money or wealth or even for more wishes. So make your wishes carefully. Remember that you are not alone in this world."

The young man frowned. That was a rather foolish thing for a bottle to say. Of course, he wasn't alone in the world, but whatever did that have to do with his wishes? Never mind. He'd make his three wishes and live happily ever after.

"Wish number one," he thought, smiling. "I wish … I wish …" But at that very moment, the sun sparkled off the bottle and flashed directly into his eyes, making him momentarily blind. "Oh drat!" he grumbled, "I wish that darn sun would stay out of my eyes!"

Suddenly the sun disappeared behind a big, black cloud and the voice in the bottle said plainly, "You have two wishes left. Remember that you are not alone in the world. Make your wishes carefully."

Just as the now-a-bit-upset young man was about to make his second wish, his dear mother and sweet sister arrived. They had spent all day tromping through the woods, looking for him, so were not in the best of moods until they saw the bottle.

"A wishing bottle!" the mother exclaimed.

"I will make a wish," cried the sister.

"No, I will," said the mother.

Before the young man could utter a single word, the two began shrieking and screaming—each trying to outtalk the other in her bid for a wish. They ranted and raved! They harassed him. They hit upon his arms and back. Angrily, the young man shouted, "Stop it, both of you. Oh, how I wish you'd both be quiet so I could think!"

"You have one wish left," said the voice from the bottle, sounding quite loud in the eerie silence surrounding the shocked threesome.

The now-soundless mother started shaking her hands in the air and screaming silently until her face got terribly red and she looked about to explode. The muted sister started hitting her brother even harder and opening and closing her mouth like a bird demanding food. "Oh honestly," the young man shouted, "you two are driving me insane. Sometimes, I wish none of us had been born." He thought he heard just a tinkle of a giggle from the bottle before suddenly everything ceased to be.

The Three Wishes — *continued*

Several years later, a wise elder came upon the same blue-green bottle hidden in the same hollow tree. He smiled. He'd heard of such bottles. He suspected he knew its purpose so wasn't at all surprised when the clear voice told him he had three wishes.

"I am a happy man," he said to himself, "and I want to stay that way. So, my first wish is for this lovely day to continue until nightfall. My second wish is for a little rain to fall tonight to freshen up the trees." He smiled to himself. He already knew it was going to rain that night, because here in this faraway land it rained *every* night.

Then he polished the bottle with his sleeve and looked at his reflection. He was certainly old. His face was full of wrinkles and laugh lines. His hair was gray and his beard was long. But his life had been good and he could not wish for anything more. Finally, he said, "and for my third wish, I wish that you would never be found by a living soul again."

For a moment nothing happened, then the voice from the bottle said, "I do not understand. Of course, your wish will be granted, but … why?"

"Well," the elder mumbled, "there is danger in wishing because too often foolish people wish only for themselves. They do not realize that to be happy, one must think first of others, of friends, of relatives, and, indeed, of all the people everywhere. For if others are happy, we will be happy too. Our happiness is intertwined with the happiness of all other living things. If the trees are unhappy and die—so will we. If the animals of the forests are unhappy and disappear—so will we. If our loved ones cry—so do we. But if they are happy—so are we. We are not alone in the world, but too often we forget that and don't act with that in mind. So, if I wish you out of existence, then no foolish humans, like myself, can be tempted to make silly wishes that could hurt many people."

"Yes," replied the clear voice from the bottle. "That was my message too. Thank you, dear elder, for no longer must I fill the selfish wishes of people who think only of themselves. Now I, too, am free."

And with that, the blue-green bottle disappeared in a pouf of smoke, and the elder strolled slowly on his away, enjoying the sun and anticipating with pleasure the rain that would fall that night.

Noteworthy Names

What's in a name? That which we call a rose, by any other name—just wouldn't be the same!

What This Project Addresses

- data gathering and processing
- organization and presentation
- creativity
- independent work
- curriculum connections: Language Arts, Health, Social Studies

Project Overview

Names again! In "People Puzzle" I noted the importance of knowing and celebrating names. Teachers are well aware of the importance of quickly learning all their students' names and of calling every student by the *correct* name. "Noteworthy Names" takes the whole "importance of names" matter a bit further. It invites the students to find out as much as possible about their individual names and then use this information to create wonderful, alphabet-type name books, based on what they have discovered.

Don't be fooled into thinking that the "alphabet-book" nature of the project will "turn off" the older students. Quite the opposite is true. Even Grade 9 students thoroughly enjoy "Noteworthy Names" and find many recipients for their completed books, often making several copies.

Students begin by researching their own *first* names. Once they have learned all they can about them through their parents and so on, they organize all their findings into book format. The idea of preparing the book in "alphabet" form adds an interesting, unique dimension to the project. It takes a familiar concept and makes it both authentic and meaningful, especially if an audience, perhaps parents or seniors, has been predetermined for the books. And because the basic theme of the books—students' names—is so important to them, I have never seen a student who was not intrinsically motivated to complete the project.

TINY TRUE TALE

"Can I change me name?" Mikey asked.

"No," laughed the teacher. "Why would you want to?"

Waving a "Names for Baby" book in his hand, Mikey replied, "'cause it says here Michael means like an angel, and we both know that's not me!"

"Actually, Mikey," the teacher whispered so only he could hear, "I think you are like an angel in many ways. Why just yesterday I saw you helping Derek with his math."

Mikey grumbled a bit, but looked pleased, and immediately wrote "I am Michael and I am sort of like an angel—sometimes."

Materials

- questionnaires
- writing materials

- small pieces of paper for books
- heavy paper for covers
- coils (or other suitable means of putting the books together)
- baby "names" books (but these work only for common, Anglo-Saxon/European names)
- overhead of Appendix E
- sample alphabet book (optional)

Steps for Teachers

One way to introduce this project is to begin with the fun activity outlined in Appendix E, where students "rename" themselves in a silly way.

1. Using an overhead of the appendix, take about ten minutes for a hilarious sharing of new names.
2. Cut regular 8 by 11 paper into quarters, and have students use them either vertically or horizontally for their book pages—the "mini-book" concept is intriguing to them. Cover pages will need to be the same size or slightly larger.
3. Following the warm-up, discuss the importance of names and especially celebrate non-dominant culture names.
4. Invite students to take home the questionnaires and fill in as much as possible with parents, relatives, or friends.
5. If you have one, share the sample alphabet book, or discuss what an alphabet book looks like. Invite students to make their own books, where they write something about their names (or about themselves if a particular letter doesn't work) for each letter of the alphabet. Do a few examples together, using your name.
6. Once the books have been completed, encourage students to share them in sharing circles or small groups, so that all can appreciate the names (and the work) of their peers.

Quick Check: Noteworthy Names

- Do all the students have enough data to make into books or do I need to "supplement"?

Steps for Students

1. Students find out as much as possible about their names, using the questionnaire as a starting point.
2. Using all the information they have gathered, they divide the facts up so that they can write one interesting piece of information to match each letter of the alphabet.
3. Once they have something for every letter of the alphabet, they neatly print one letter and the facts that match it on each of the small pages. Students will end up with 26 pages—one for every letter of the alphabet. Here is an example from the book of a boy called Michael. Notice how he tied the "A" into his name. He couldn't fit the letter "B" directly to his name, so he found another word, "boy," that started with that letter, and made it work.

A: Angel
*Michael means like an **a**ngel. I didn't think I was like that until my teacher showed me that sometimes I was.*
   1.

B: Boy
*I am a **B**oy called Mikey. I like being a boy.*
   2.

G: Great Grandfather
My mom said I was named after my **G**reat **G**randfather who was called Charles Michael.
   7.

L: Like
I really **L**ike my name. I wouldn't change it except maybe to Rocky.
   12.

Z:
My name is Mikey, but if I put a "c" in it, it is Mickey, and that rhymes with the letter "**Z**."
   26.

4. Students may add pictures, illustrations, and colored backgrounds. Once all the pages are finished, they make covers and ensure that their names appear there. They also fasten their books together and include their author signatures.

Dealing with Diversities

Cultural: These students often have names that may seem unusual to the western culture children. Here they are asked to show off these wonderful names, and in sharing circles, to tell about them.

Socio-economic: If any students are not living with birth parents, but rather in group or foster homes, make an attempt to contact the guardian(s) and help the children find out as much as possible. In some cases you may need to be "creative" in order to help these students find out about their names. (*Your name sounds a lot like ___; perhaps it means ___*)

Gifted: Encourage these students to do a more in-depth research about their given names or to write their alphabet books in rhyme, with metaphors, or in any other fashion that interests and excites them.

Dealing with Developmental Levels

Kindergarten to Grade 3: Keep it simple. You may need to go through the alphabet together and list a few words beginning with each letter. Students can use this as a word bank when creating their pages. I *have* seen this used effectively by a Grade 1 class, albeit it took a long time to complete.

Grades 4 to 9: Teacher enthusiasm is key here, as some students may feel "insulted" to be making alphabet books. However, once they start compiling their data and trying to fit it on the pages, they'll realize the project is not as easy as they thought.

Making Curriculum Connections and More

Language Arts: Among the options are comparing different books and names using graphic organizers and writing "alliteration names" where, in small groups, students write an alliterative sentence for each person in another group (e.g., *Mysterious Melanie makes merry music*) then share them as a class. Fun! Students may also write diamante poems about themselves and another person with the same name. (This formula poem creates an excellent visual comparison.)

Diamante Poem

Noun (*Your name*)
Two adjectives that describe the first noun (*you*)
Three *ing* verbs that tell what you like to do
Two nouns associated with the first noun (*you*), two nouns associated
with the second noun (*other person*)
Three *ing* verbs that tell what the other noun (*person*) likes to do
Two adjectives that describe the second noun (*person*)
Second noun (*person*)

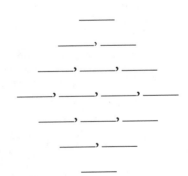

Health: Here is an opportunity to learn about self and family.

Social Studies: Students may discover more about their historical roots and ancestors. They could learn about family trees, perhaps actually making one.

Noteworthy Names Questionnaire

To Ask Relatives

1. Was I named after anyone, and if so, who and why? If not, why did you choose my name?

    _____

2. What does my name mean?

    _____

3. Is there a cultural background to my name?

    _____

To Ask Yourself

1. Do I like my name? Why or why not?

    _____

2. If I had to change my first name, what would I change it to? Why?

    _____

3. Do I know any famous person with the same first name as I have? If so, who? Do I like or dislike that person?

    _____

4. If a movie was going to be made about me, who would I want to have playing me?

    _____

5. Does my name ever show up on TV, in songs, in commercials? When and how?

    _____

6. Do I have a nickname? If so what is it and how do I feel about it?

    _____

7. What nickname would I like to have? Why?

    _____

8. Do I know how to say my name in any other language? If so, what is it?

    _____

Story Theatre Presentations

We will draw the curtain and show you the picture.

What This Project Addresses

- listening and speaking
- memorization
- comprehension of literature
- reading for fluency
- self-confidence and sense of self
- dramatization
- curriculum connections: Language Arts, Health, Social Studies, Drama

Project Overview

Children are natural actors! Think of them on the playground, or playing "house" or "school" or "cowboy." They are uninhibited and amazingly creative, and yet we seldom give them a chance to show this off in the school setting. Story Theatre provides that opportunity, as well as the opportunity for considerable laughter and enjoyment.

I include this project, although it differs considerably from the others, because it is such an original, and often overlooked or misunderstood variation on the familiar Readers Theatre. I feel it offers *so much more* in the way of enjoyment and opportunities for learning.

Some of you may remember *Story Theatre*, a popular television show from about twenty years ago. This project loosely follows the format of that show. Basically, it is a way to *read* or *memorize* a familiar story so that it is presented *exactly* the way it is written. For example, the tag words (words that explain who is speaking in a direct quotation, such as *said Brian*, or *answered Susan*) are spoken aloud. So are all the thoughts and actions. This is what makes the presentation so much fun. The actors actually say everything. Confused? Scan Appendix F for a spoof of Little Red Riding Hood written as Story Theatre. You will soon understand the concept, and trust me, students catch on to it more quickly than adults do.

Break any short story that the class has read into sections, according to what character is predominant in each section, and have the student who *represents* that character read, and act out at the same time, *every word*. As an example, if the wolf is hiding in the woods, he will move stealthily through imaginary trees while saying, "*The big, bad wolf snuck through the trees with a hungry look in his eyes. He saw a little girl and said, 'hello, little girl, where are you going?'*" Students love this idea and have so much fun with it. And what's more: it can make a wonderful presentation for a school concert!

The basic guidelines for Story Theatre are as follows:

- Characters speak of themselves in third person.
- Characters *say* what they are doing as they *do* it.
- Characters act and speak the narrative at the same time.
- Actions specific to a character are spoken by that character. Example: As the *Ogress began pulling* … the child screamed …

- A narrator can be used to keep the story moving smoothly or to "read" lengthy parts, but should be unnecessary as characters can *tell* the actions, thoughts, and setting.
- Characters say as well as *show* feelings and thoughts.
- Characters do a lot of mime while talking.
- Words that indicate a direct quotation are said together with the quotation, for example, "Let me in," *she cried*.
- Use of costume pieces is advisable.
- Provide practice time to encourage reading fluency.

An interesting side benefit to taking part in "Story Theatre Presentations" is that it enables students to write direct quotations better, complete with perfect punctuation—a difficult feat for many. I think this happens because of the extra focus placed on the tag words themselves.

TINY TRUE TALE

Note received at the end of a school year.

Dear Mrs. X,
The most fun I had this year was doing that story theatre thing. It was a lot of fun and I learned to read real good by being the wolf. I was a shy kid until I did the wolf. Now I'm not so bad. And I like reading more too. I hope I get to do stuff like that next year too.
Thanks for making it fun to read.
Your friend, __

Materials

- any interesting short story—the more characters the better (although students can be inanimate objects too)
- highlighters for students to mark their parts
- props, such as hats and masks, which you have in the room

Steps for Teachers

To introduce "Story Theatre Presentations," model a few lines of a story yourself, drawing attention to the tag words and pointing out that the characters don't say those words, but how funny it would be if they did.

1. Select a story carefully, break it into manageable chunks, and assign a "character" to each chunk, or use the Story Theatre sample included as Appendix F.
2. For at least the first time, assign parts according to whom you think will best be able to handle and demonstrate the technique. (After the first time, everyone will want to be involved.)
3. Allow lots of practice time to promote fluency and self-confidence.
4. Arrange for students to present to the class first and then to neighboring classes.

Quick Check: Story Theatre Presentations

- Are there parts of the story that do not readily transpose to a particular character, and if so, how can I deal with them? (Having a narrator or a speaking inanimate object such as a nearby tree are options.)
- Do I have an assortment of props? (Local second-hand stores are a great resource for these.)

Steps for Students

1. Students read the whole story together in small groups, either silently or with one person reading and the rest following.
2. Students read their own sections many times until they feel comfortable with them. They may memorize their parts or portions of their parts, but do not have to. It is all right for them to have paper in their hands and read the lines, while carrying out the actions as they read.
3. Each group begins saying their lines and acting out what they are saying at the same time. There is no right or wrong way to do this. The main thing is to have fun with the story. Props may be added.
4. The groups present their stories to the class and perhaps another audience.

Dealing with Diversities

Linguistic: Although these students may not understand all (or even any) of the language, they still enjoy being involved. If you give them a short section, they will gain an excellent opportunity to learn or practise the language.

Intellectual: Sometimes these students have trouble understanding the concept of Story Theatre until they see it demonstrated, so start with very small parts for them, or allow them non-speaking parts, such as playing background music, until they feel comfortable. Aim to involve these students totally while maintaining a low-risk environment.

Physical: Children with physical challenges often make the best actors in Story Theatre simply because they *say* what they are doing, even if they can't actually do it.

Gifted: Challenge these students to take a story and prepare it as Story Theatre by breaking it into parts or rewriting it as is done in Appendix F.

Dealing with Developmental Levels

Kindergarten to Grade 3: Use very simple stories (e.g., Chicken Little) that the students already know and allow them to improvise as well as read what they can.

Grades 4 to 9: Once they get the knack of Story Theatre, encourage them to find their own stories and work them into appropriate scripts. Remember that rewriting is unnecessary as long as they can break the stories up according to characters.

Making Curriculum Connections and More

Language Arts: Students may practise writing conversations with appropriate punctuation or identifying both direct and indirect quotations in literature. They may write original scripts for Story Theatre or adapt existing stories. As far as their presentations go, they could create posters, write invitations to families, staff members, and community member to attend, or write about their feelings when performing in Story Theatre presentations.

Health: Extensions include discussing the positive effects of human interactions on personal development and considering how to contribute to a community, such as clubs and groups.

Social Studies: Students could take the opportunity to research and discuss the role of theatre in history or act out events from history in Story Theatre fashion.

2 Projects That Emphasize Application

Application is the first of what Bloom terms the *higher level objectives*. At this level of thinking, students are asked to apply what they have learned to their own lives or to specific conditions provided by the teacher. Basically, they transfer learning to new situations; they apply abstract ideas in concrete situations to problem-solve where there is generally a "best" or "single" response.

Student success in this area is usually measured by the extent to which a problem is solved and by the depth of the means used to solve it. Questions beginning with "Give a personal example … " or "What do you think … " reflect this level of thinking.

It is assumed that projects listed in this section of the book cover the skills incorporated in Knowledge and Comprehension, but also call for many of the Application skills. The following summarizes the main Application skill clusters for each project in this chapter.

Class Mosaic: Students will select, modify, and organize personal symbols and images in order to demonstrate and illustrate pertinent facts about themselves.

Historical Figures: Students will collect pertinent facts and then manipulate materials so as to construct informative representations of heritage costumes.

Fortune Cookie Wishes: Students will discover important facts about themselves and others; then, after determining the possible needs of others, they will organize and prepare appropriate fortunes.

Super Hero Posters: Students will classify, categorize, and imagine traits of a super hero, prior to constructing and illustrating their ideas.

The Money Tree: Students will utilize prior knowledge about money and will, through careful observation of others, discover, predict, and interpret the effects of positive remarks and peer support.

Marvelous Masks of Many Colors: Students will demonstrate and inform by selecting and manipulating materials in order to create imaginative representations of themselves.

Innovative Instruments: Students will experiment, select, and modify in order to prepare imaginative instruments that they can share with peers.

Class Mosaic

Let's go hand in hand—not one before the other.

What This Project Addresses

- cultural awareness and celebration of diversity
- symbolism (optional)
- the importance of individuals as being "part of a whole," class cohesiveness, and class pride
- creativity, self-concept, and personal identification
- participation skills
- curriculum connections: Language Arts, Health, Social Studies, Mathematics, Art

Project Overview

When you look around your classroom and see everyone doing something different, don't you sometimes wonder at the magnificent mosaic before your eyes? One definition of mosaic is a decorative design made by inlaying small pieces. The purpose of "Class Mosaic" is for students to recognize that they are all a part of one big universe of people *and* all a part of one class. This project calls for students to create "tiles" that will express something personal about themselves and then to add their tiles to a big circle that represents the entire class. When all the tiles are attached to a large background and the finished product proudly displayed, everyone will experience a profound sense of pride and involvement. Students of all ages are thrilled to see the finished product, and the day of the "unveiling" never ceases to be exciting for everyone.

TINY TRUE TALE

The girl stood in front of the completed class mosaic, her eyes wide with appreciation. "It's beautiful," she whispered to the boy beside her.

He was in a wheelchair. Although the cerebral palsy from which he suffered made it almost impossible for him to control the erratic movements of his arms, he spoke and thought clearly. "Yes," he said proudly, "and there I am right in the middle of the group." He gestured wildly to his tile, so wonderfully decorated with a splashy array of colors vaguely resembling a rainbow—typical of his irrepressible optimism. The girl smiled at him and patted his shoulder.

I watched silently, wondering how infrequently that particular boy felt "right in the middle of the group." I vowed to be more aware in the future.

Materials

- large circular piece of paper, about 1.5 m to 2 m in diameter
- large scissors for cutting out individual tiles
- small individual tiles, one per student
- information on symbolism, if desired
- white glue

Discuss how each class member is different and has unique interests and capabilities. Share some of your own likes and skills with the class. Have the class consider how people demonstrate their uniqueness. Introduce the concept of mosaic and then talk about personal tiles as single pieces of a mosaic. If possible, share pictures of mosaics.

- coloring mediums, such as felt pens, crayons, pastels, and pencil crayons
- magazines for collages or any other "decorating" supplies
- pictures of mosaics (if possible)

Steps for Teachers

1. Tape two pieces of metre-wide paper from a roll, then cut into a circle approximately 1.5 m to 2 m in diameter. Paint this "background" any dark color with poster paint.
2. Cut a second circle the same size as the first. Divide it into parts by folding in half, then quarters, then eighths. Open the second circle and draw a small circle in the centre (about 30 cm in diameter) and another circle about halfway from the centre point. (See Figure 10.)
3. Cut up the divided portions to make one "tile" per student. (**Note:** If you have too many tiles, offer them to students who want to make more than one.) (See Figure 11.) The tiles do not have to be in a uniform pattern. As long as there is a piece for each student, that is good enough. Figure 11 is simply one possible design.
4. Mark the *back* of each tile with an "X." (Students do *not* color this side.)
5. Decorate the small centre circle yourself to use as a model, or simply label it with the class name.
6. Introduce the concept of *symbol* (something that represents or stands for something else), if desired. You might make this a separate lesson in which the symbols of other cultures are examined, or with younger children, omit the component.
7. Invite students to decorate individual tiles in any way that represents them. For example, they might show favorite colours, activities, and foods.
8. Collect tiles and have students help you glue them to the black background.

Class Mosaic

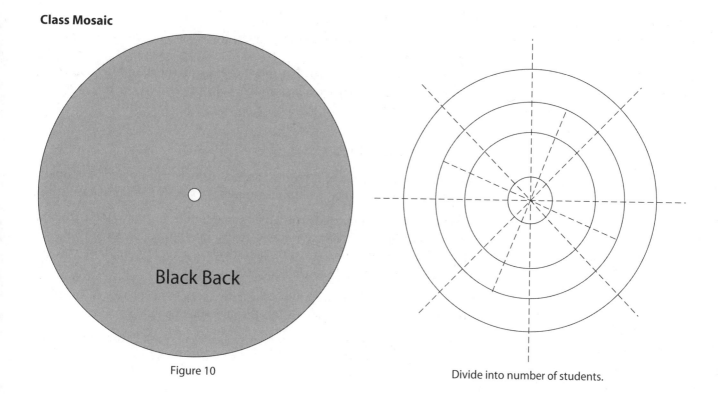

Figure 10

Divide into number of students.

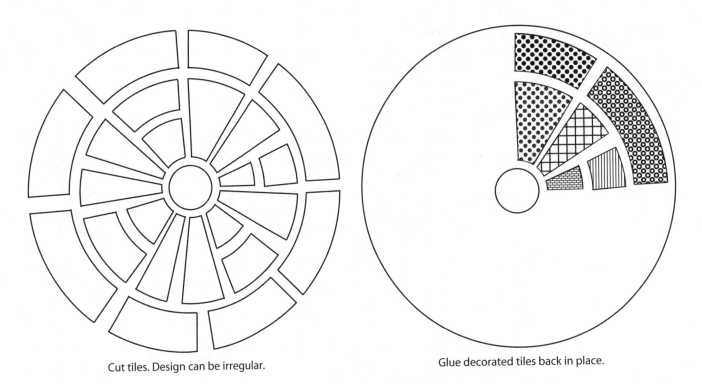

Cut tiles. Design can be irregular.

Glue decorated tiles back in place.

Figure 11

Quick Check: Class Mosaic

- Do I have each piece marked with an "X" on the back?
- Are there enough decorating materials for all students?
- Do I have enough white glue for attaching the tiles to the background?

Steps for Students

1. Students determine what colors, shapes, items, and activities *tell about*, or symbolize them.
2. They decorate their tiles so that they are very personal and say something about them. They may use illustrations, cut-out pictures, writing, whatever helps represent them.

Dealing with Diversities

Cultural: Encourage use of symbols specific to their cultures, for example, a menorah for Jewish culture, a lotus blossom for Japanese, a shamrock for Irish.

Linguistic: Use the completed centre tile as an example. Encourage ESL students to work beside peers so that any students struggling with the dominant language will quickly get the idea. Encourage these students to include a couple of words on their tiles written in their home languages.

Physical: Alternative tile decorating suggestions include collages of magazine pictures, photographs, and hand prints through finger paint.

Socio-economic: Provide coloring mediums as they may not have a variety available.

Behavioral: Invite students to help you make the large background circle and then help glue.

Gifted: Invite these students to include a personal poem or meaningful quotations on their tiles.

Dealing with Developmental Levels

Kindergarten to Grade 3: Encourage drawing, collage techniques, or even abstract coloring, on individual tiles. Keep the tile shapes simple.

Grades 4 to 9: Encourage more written material—poetry, quotes, symbolism, or meaningful messages—on individual tiles.

Making Curriculum Connections and More

Language Arts: Students may discuss or write reflections on their tiles and the finished mosaic. They could write questions about the mosaic, exercising higher levels of thinking, for example: "Compare it to …What feelings does it invoke …? The project could become the subject of news articles for the school paper or newsletter. Students could also create graphic organizers comparing tiles, review the procedure involved in creating the mosaic, and write invitations to the principal, families, and more to see the mosaic.

Health: Related topics include "fitting in" and being part of a group, as well as the importance and beauty of individualism, which could be examined through discussion.

Social Studies: The class could research mosaics and their significance in history and find examples of art mosaics in different cultures, including modern North American culture. It might be interesting for students to compare pictures of mosaics from books with those they have created.

Mathematics: Related ideas include examining parts and wholes, and exploring fractions and geometry (circles, diameter). Students could use mathematical tools such as compass and rule to create small individual mosaics.

Historical Figures

What This Project Addresses

- cultural diversity
- creativity and artistry
- independent and group work
- class cohesiveness
- personal similarities and differences
- curriculum connections: Language Arts, Social Studies, Art

Project Overview

It has been my experience that even today's high-tech kids enjoy creating garments for paper figures.

Every teacher faces the problem of students' apparel in class, especially if there are a few children from diverse cultures whose traditional clothing does not "fit the norm." One unique way to deal with this, or just to increase awareness of cultural diversity and view it as a beautiful resource as opposed to a problem, is to encourage close examination of the manner in which different people around the globe dress. Since all students at some point in their historic backgrounds come from another country, tracing roots and examining the traditional clothing found there can be both enlightening and exciting.

The goal of "Historical Figures" is to have students "dress" paper figures in the manner of their cultural backgrounds. Hence a boy whose ancestors were from the Scottish highlands might dress the figure in a kilt, whereas a girl with grandparents still living in Japan might dress the doll in a kimono. This provides students with a visual representation of their unique histories. The paper figures can be dressed with drawings, fabric swatches, pieces cut out from magazines, and so on.

The first time I introduced this, I was unsure about how some of the boys in the Grade 6 class would react, but found that the project got overwhelmingly positive responses. (I did have a few dolls dressed in black leather, but that was the apparel of a popular rock band at the time.) I fully believe that if the teacher shows enthusiasm for the activity, the students will be enthusiastic as well. Consequently, I suggest that you dress a doll appropriately and use it as a model at the outset of the project. I dressed my doll in a piece of green felt (I am from Ireland), poorly cut to resemble a dress, glued a few paper shamrocks on it, and put a paper, plaid shawl around the shoulders. One student said sweetly, "That's very nice, Ms. P. but is that the *best* you could do?"

Younger students especially need help "discovering their roots," so be sure to send a letter home explaining the task.

Note: Remember to call the dolls "figures" so as to avoid "poo-pooing" by older students. The final dressed *figures* can be posted on the wall, parade fashion, as a beautiful, visual reminder of our many differences.

Jessie didn't want to "dress a dumb doll." He was ten years old and "not about to do anything so stupid." He was told by the teacher he didn't have to, and his doll representative could certainly be placed in the parade with just his name written on it, because, after all, he was an important member of the class so his representative couldn't be left out. However, when the finished products began arriving—the Aboriginal boy's doll striking in a traditional outfit and feather headdress (made with real feathers), the Ukrainian girl's doll in a colorful apron, the Irish girl's doll in a green paper dress covered with shamrocks, and the Mexican boy's doll (none of us even knew David was of Mexican ancestry) dressed in a colorful little cloth serape made with his grandmother's help, and a paper Mexican hat, Jessie's unadorned doll looked rather foolish in the parade. He quietly took it down and the next day it reappeared dressed in full RCMP regalia. (His guardian had helped him to draw the outfit at home.) Until that time, we never knew Jessie had an uncle in the Royal Canadian Mounted Police.

Materials

- paper doll cut-outs on firm backing
- glues, bits of cloth, any other "notions," such as mini hats, you can find from dollar stores
- magazines, especially ones that have examples of around-the-world costumes that students can cut from (e.g., *National Geographic*)
- a variety of coloring mediums and paper
- scissors, tape, needles, thread, and safety pins
- a range of pictures/posters of ethnic costumes

Steps for Teachers

1. Dress a doll according to your ancestry. Try to use both paper and fabric in the outfit.
2. Prepare one figure outline for each class member.
3. Introduce the concept of traditional or national "costumes." Share your own ethnic background and "costume." For example, if Scottish, you could wear a kilt. Or try to bring a piece of a costume if you cannot put together an entire outfit. For example, wearing a Mexican sombrero (if you are of Latino heritage) or a babushka (if Ukrainian) helps to set the scene.
4. Explain the project and invite students to look at your already "dressed" paper figure. Ensure that students understand how the "costumes" can be made out of whatever the students want, ranging from paper to fabric pieces.
5. Share as many pictures as you have, and discuss ethnic backgrounds. Many students will say "Canadian" or "American" and not realize they have other ancestry. In the event that some students cannot (or will not) research their heritage, allow them to dress their figures in typically North American fashion.
6. It is a good idea to begin the activity in class and then allow students to take the figures home to get parental help. However, since some students cannot or will not take them home, it remains important to provide class time.

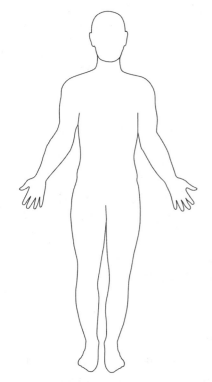

You will want a basic figure at least large enough for an 8 by 11 page.

Figure 12

Quick Check: Historical Figures

- Have I arranged for sufficient help for students?
- Do I need to contact parents ahead of time to ask for input?
- Are there community members, such as dressmakers and artists, whom I might call upon for help?
- Do I have a good model, or sample of my own heritage, ready?

Steps for Students

1. Students find out about their heritage, going as far back as possible, by talking to parents, relatives, and grandparents. They either ask about or research traditional costumes, perhaps with teacher help.
2. Once they have decided how to dress their figures, they gather the necessary materials.
3. Students dress their figures, giving them faces, if they want to.

Dealing with Diversities

Cultural: This is where these students will shine. Allow them total freedom.

Linguistic: It will probably be unnecessary to use an interpreter to describe the project because your demonstration will make the task clear, but spend some one-on-one time with students to clarify, if necessary.

Physical: Ensure aide assistance, if necessary. You may be able to use a class peer who could be described as Gifted to help in this case.

Socio-economic: Be sure to have lots of decorating materials available.

Gifted: Encourage these students to do research to discover tiny details of heritage costumes and to add these to their dolls. These students may also like researching disappearing traditions of specific cultures that make up the national mosaic.

Dealing with Developmental Levels

Kindergarten to Grade 3: You may need to solicit help from parents, aides, and older students for this project, but the effort will be well worth the time involved. Have the figures already attached to firm backing.

Grades 4 to 9: Encourage more creative use of fabric, buttons, and notions of every kind. Exploring various traditional cultural outfits before beginning the doll decoration helps to stimulate creativity.

Making Curriculum Connections and More

Language Arts: The many options include writing descriptions of personal traditional costumes, writing about what students like and dislike about their traditional outfits, writing about themselves in the outfits, and discussing or writing about how class members are all much the same, but come from different backgrounds.

Social Studies: The class could discuss the history and use of ceremonial, traditional dress or research disappearing traditions.

"Historical Figures" is an excellent project to do in anticipation of an Open House. A row of historically garbed figures outside your room on a wall or window creates a colorful representation of all the diverse students in your classroom.

Fortune Cookie Wishes

Our remedies oft in ourselves do lie.

What This Project Addresses

- cultural diversity
- responsibility for actions taken
- respect, appreciation, and affection
- appreciation of the needs of others
- effective communication for expression of feelings
- curriculum connections: Language Arts, Health

Project Overview

Who doesn't like opening fortune cookies? There's a certain thrill in reading a fortune that is usually so ridiculous that there's no way it could ever fit. Right? Yet we still scramble to choose the perfect cookie from the plate. Students feel the same way, and as smart teachers, we can make use of this awareness. As well, students love to give little gifts, and "Fortune Cookie Wishes" allows them to do that. Often, the biggest problem is in limiting the number of cookies that students make.

This particular project gives students an easy vehicle for showing appreciation. Showing sincere feelings of gratitude to or affection for others doesn't come easily to all children. Here, they can "show it with a cookie." This action can also serve as a catalyst for many subsequent activities about human needs and relationships.

The special fortune cookies are made by first writing a fortune specifically for a special person, wrapping the slip of paper in plastic wrap, and placing it between two flat cookies that will be stuck together with icing. The finished products make excellent Mother's Day or Father's Day gifts, or just tokens of general appreciation.

TINY TRUE TALE

One young lady, Jill, had been sitting for a very long time with a blank piece of paper in front of her. "I don't know what to write," she grumbled. "This is dumb! I got nothing to say to her." Jill's task was to write a short "good fortune" for someone special, whom she had decided would be her stepmom as there "was no one else."

The teacher whispered that she was sure something would come to her, and if it didn't, she was just to create the sandwich cookie without the fortune. The next time the teacher checked, Jill was busily wrapping the "completed" cookie in plastic and putting it in her backpack. Since it was obvious Jill had no intention of sharing the fortune she had written, if, in fact, she had written one, the teacher dismissed the issue.

*The next morning the teacher opened her e-mail to find a brief note from Jill's stepmother. The note said, "Thank you so much. The fortune said **I love you, mom. Thanks for loving me.** I never even knew she cared. I am crying right now."*

Materials

- fortune cookies
- round, flat cookies, such as Digestive cookies, enough for at least two per child
- cans of icing—one can fills about fifteen cookies.
- small pieces of paper for writing fortunes
- plastic wrap

Steps for Teachers

1. Let students open fortune cookies and then discuss the fortunes with questions such as *Does this fit for you? Is it a silly fortune? Would it work for anyone?*
2. Discuss ways to show affection with significant people. Brainstorm for ways to tell them how others feel about them.
3. Discuss individual differences and why different people require different things and, consequently, different fortunes or "good wishes."
4. Encourage students to choose a significant person in their lives, write as many warm wishes as they can, and then choose the best one to transfer onto the "fortune paper."

Quick Check: Fortune Cookie Wishes

- Do I have enough fortune cookies for at least one per student? (Often packages contain broken cookies; no one wants a broken one.)
- Have I pre-checked the students' chosen "fortunes" before they "hide" them in the icing?

Steps for Students

1. Students open their cookies, talk about their fortunes, and then decide who they would like to give a "good fortune" to.
2. Students write several possible good fortunes or warm wishes for someone, making sure that they will be authentic and meaningful for that person.
3. They pick their favorite and print it neatly on the small paper, fold the paper, and wrap it tightly in plastic wrap. They then stick two cookies together with icing and put the plastic-wrapped fortune in the middle with the icing.
4. Once the whole cookie is wrapped in plastic, it is given to the intended person.

Dealing with Diversities

Cultural: Encourage these students to write fortunes according to any cultural beliefs, guidelines, or understandings familiar to them.

Linguistic: Let ESL students write in their first language. Make use of a tutor or interpreter, if necessary.

Religious: Some religions frown upon gift giving. If this is the case with any students, suggest that they write letters of appreciation instead (but allow them to make *fortuneless* cookies for themselves).

Motivational and Behavioral: Allow them to make the cookies minus fortunes if they balk at writing fortunes for others, or suggest that they write fortunes for themselves.

Pass out the mass-produced kind of fortune cookie, one per student, and invite the students to open the cookies and talk about their fortunes. Once you have steered the discussion toward showing appreciation of others, tell the class that you will provide an excellent way for them to show appreciation to a special person.

Gifted: Perhaps these students could include a quote or short poem with their fortunes.

Dealing with Developmental Levels

Kindergarten to Grade 3: If students are too young to write fortunes, partner them with older students who will act as scribes. The small size of the paper to put in the cookies will prohibit drawing, but these children truly love the activity. It takes only a few minutes for an older partner or student to write out a younger child's words.

Grades 4 to 9: Encouraging specificity of comments is important. This helps students to understand how people's needs differ.

Making Curriculum Connections and More

Language Arts: The class could brainstorm the many ways significant people in their lives help them, and then write about this. They could also role-play situations where appreciation of others is shown, write personal reflections about giving their fortune cookies, or make posters about kindness and appreciation.

Health: "Fortune Cookie Wishes" could lead into discussions about the importance of sharing feelings or when it's best not to share them (to strangers). Students could also compile lists of different ways to show or say "I love you" or "Thank you."

Social Studies: The class could take an opportunity to discuss how different cultures show appreciation (e.g., in Cree thanks is implied from actions, not expressed through words). Students could also learn about polite behavior in different cultures from one another. For example, in First Nations and Asian cultures, it is not polite to make eye contact when talking.

Super Hero Posters

We are such stuff as dreams are made of.

What This Project Addresses

- creativity, imagination
- representation and visualization
- listening
- organization
- shared effort and cooperation
- group-work skills
- curriculum connections: Language Arts, Health, Social Studies, Science, Art, Drama

Project Overview

Everyone loves a super hero. This project allows students to use some of their unexploited creativity to create their very own super heroes, and they love it. They will be amazed when you tell them their *assignment* is to create a super hero.

After researching heroes and discussing super heroes, groups work together to create their imaginary super heroes—male or female—according to the grade-specific conditions provided by you. (See **Dealing with Developmental Levels**.)

The finished products are wonderful wall posters that not only decorate the room, but are the jumping-off points for many additional curriculum-based activities.

TINY TRUE TALE

Jason did very little in class other than doodle on his books and papers and daydream. When put into groups for the "Super Hero" project, his group instantly made him the "official artist." Although there was much more to the task than the actual drawing of the character, Jason's role became dominant and he excelled. His group's creation was so amazing, due in great part to Jason's artistic skill, that they ended up "taking their show on the road," by sharing the poster and accompanying story with neighboring classes.

It would be great to report that Jason's in-class behavior improved dramatically as a result of his new-found status. It didn't. He continued to doodle and daydream his time away, but at least he had enjoyed a few minutes of fame.

The truly remarkable thing happened several years later when I heard from Jason. He was taking a commercial art course and doing well in it, and (yeah!) his favorite illustrations were those he drew of—you guessed it—super heroes!

The fact that he contacted me to tell me he still remembered the "Super Hero" project from seven years before had **some** *merit as far as I was concerned!*

Materials

- comics, posters, overheads, or cartoons of super heroes
- large poster paper (the heavier and sturdier the better)
- a variety of drawing/coloring mediums
- magazines that can be cut up
- scissors
- white glue
- fabric scraps, buttons, feathers, and any assorted odds and ends you can find
- video or DVD of any super hero (optional)
- Group Roles chart, one per group and one per student

To introduce the project, have a discussion about students' favorite super heroes. You may even want to begin this by showing a few minutes of a video or DVD featuring a super hero, or by sharing poems, stories, or pictures as needed for motivation. Then, discuss the differences between super heroes and real-life heroes as preparation for inviting students to discuss super heroes and possibly real-life heroes in groups.

Steps for Teachers

1. Locate any short stories, poems, or pictures pertaining to heroes in general. Most reading series have several pieces of text that would fit the criteria. In addition, newspapers and good magazines often highlight heroic actions. Of course, the most common resource will be comic books; invite students to bring in any they may have. Share these resources with students before they get into groups.
2. Form student groups, making sure that there are a variety of strengths in each group. Consider diversities when grouping.
3. Make one copy of the Group Roles chart for each group plus one for each student.

Quick Check: Super Hero Posters

- Do I have a variety of resources that illustrate super heroes in case some children do not understand the concept or have access to such materials?

Steps for Students

1. Once the whole-class discussion is finished, students meet in their groups and brainstorm the characteristics of a super hero.
2. In their groups, students select the traits of their own super hero and have one group member record them. They also decide on a name for the hero.
3. Each group then produces a colorful poster of its super hero, using as many different coloring tools as possible. Members may even glue pieces from magazine pictures or scraps of fabric to the poster. Everyone is expected to contribute in some way. Students are responsible for filling in the Group Roles chart correctly as they work. Each student will have a completed Group Roles chart that is different from other members of the same group. These help both you and the students understand their contributions to the group.
4. Each group labels its poster to show the abilities of its hero (e.g., an extra finger for grabbing quickly) or adds a legend at the bottom to explain all the hero's amazing qualities.

Dealing with Diversities

Cultural: Children of some cultures are not as aware of the super hero image as western world children are, but once the group gets going, these students quickly get involved. In other instances, these students may have very specific ideas about super heroes based on their cultural backgrounds; they should be encouraged to include these ideas in the group creations.

Linguistic: There will be little need for verbal explanations; they will see what is going on and be able to contribute even with minimum language.

Dealing with Developmental Levels

Kindergarten to Grade 3: It is a good idea to get very young children started by allowing them to trace one of the group members (who lies on the poster paper while others draw an outline). Another alternative is for the teacher to provide each group with a generic "gingerbread" person outlined on the poster paper. (One appears as Figure 16 under "Amazing Compilation Person.")

Grades 4 to 9: The sky's the limit here. Just give them free rein and watch the creativity at work.

Making Curriculum Connections and More

Language Arts: Follow-up opportunities include writing creative stories about the adventures of the super heroes; advice columns from a super hero's point of view; news articles about something a super hero has done, such as saving a person from a burning building; a radio talk show where a super hero is interviewed; and letters of appreciation to a real-life hero (who has influenced the student's life).

Health: This project can lead into discussions about ways in which each person is a hero, the importance of knowing personal strengths and weaknesses, and reflections on why people need heroes in their lives. Students may also make charts of "personal heroic characteristics."

Social Studies and Science: Students could research real-life heroes in both these areas.

Art: Related activities include creating comic strips or cartoons about the super heroes and making super heroes from clay or play dough.

Drama: The Hot Seat technique, whereby a student acting as the super hero is asked questions by the others and answers "in role" works well here. Students could also act out situations where the super hero does something amazing, or funny, or brave. There is also potential to create tableaux, mimes, or scripted skits involving the super heroes.

Group Roles Chart

Your group should choose a person to fill each of the following group roles. This person will be the most responsible for that part of the group's task, but everyone should help with all areas. There may be more than one person for each role.

Group Leader _____
- Is responsible for organizing the group and making sure that the group stays on task

Group Scriber _____
- Is responsible for jotting down all the brainstormed ideas and recording the specific, selected ideas about the hero; is also responsible for any printing done on the poster, for example, the name of the hero or the legend

Group Artist _____
- Is responsible for getting the drawing under way and providing the main artistic input

Group Collector _____
- Is responsible for gathering together all the materials the group will need to complete the poster and keeping them safe until the project is completed

Group Presenter _____
- Is responsible for the visual and oral presentation of the poster to the class

Think about your role in the group. Evaluate your success in each of the following areas by checking the column that best describes your work. Once you have done that, reflect in your journal on how well you work in a group, what value you got from the group work, and how you might improve your contribution to a group another time.

My role: _____

	Excellent ***	Average **	Just OK *	Not So Good
1. I did everything required of my role.				
2. I accepted my role willingly.				
3. I was able to help others in my group.				
4. I learned some things from others in my group.				
5. I had lots of good ideas.				

The Money Tree

All that glistens is not gold.

What This Project Addresses

- sharing, showing appreciation of others
- humor and merriment
- confidence
- individual and cooperative work
- curriculum connections: Language Arts, Health, Social Studies

Project Overview

If only money grew on trees! How often we hear or think that. This project capitalizes on that very idea and taps into students' imaginations and senses of humor. Beginning with a bare tree branch and some easily made "funny money," students are encouraged to write bits of humor, notes of appreciation, or general "warm fuzzies" for others on the backs of the "funny money," and hang these on the money tree. Watch the tree fill up with money. The end result is a novel adornment to your class (see Figure 13), from which many equally novel learning situations will quite naturally arise.

The Money Tree

clay

Figure 13

Claire was obviously unhappy. Her precious dog, Rascal, had just died and she was mourning. The teacher noticed another child in the Grade 6 class patting Claire on the shoulder and he overheard the second child say, "It must really hurt. I'll put a dollar on the money tree for you. You can look at it when I'm finished. It won't make Rascal come back, but it will make you laugh. OK?" Claire simply nodded.

The second child took a blank bill of "funny money" from the stack, wrote on the back of it, and hung it on the tree. Claire slowly approached the tree and read the back of the bill. She stood there for a few minutes and then smiled. She turned to her friend and said, "That's about the dumbest joke ever."

"Yep. But it made you smile," the child replied.

The teacher could hardly wait to read the "funny money" note. It read: Knock, knock. Who's there? Claire. Claire who? Claire – voyant. The girl who can see the future and knows she'll get a new puppy some day!

But the best part of the tale is that the teacher, wise capitalizer of the teachable moment that he was, immediately had the entire class think of silly "Knock knock" jokes that worked with names. Here are a few they came up with: Don – Key, Dan – Druff, Levi – Tate, Anna – Conda and Cara – Sel.

Materials

If you can't find any fake bills, simply draw a facsimile and use colored copy paper.

- tree branch with lots of smaller branches coming from it (any size you want it to be, but at least a half metre in height is good)
- lump of soft clay or putty in which to stand the tree branch
- paper or fabric to cover the lump of clay
- photocopies of any "bill" from Monolopy game–type currency
- paper clips
- box or container for the "funny money"—a shoebox works well

Steps for Teachers

You might introduce the project by asking, "Wouldn't it be nice if money grew on trees?" Discuss this as a class. Talk about how we often *buy* gifts for people to show them how we feel, but how we can show appreciation of others *without* money. Discuss the value of sharing humor and giving positive affirmations to others. Demonstrate the use of the "funny money" by writing a positive note to the principal on the back of one bill.

1. Find and stand the bare branch in your class by squishing a lump of clay or putty around the bottom of the branch. Doing this provides instant motivation for what's to come. Cover the clay with anything attractive such as a piece of felt much as a Christmas tree stand is masked if one celebrates Christmas
2. Photocopy a fake money bill on colored paper and cut out the "funny money." You could also make this a class project or the task of a volunteer or aide. Put all the cut-out "funny money" in a box or container and put a box of paper clips in the container too.
3. Discuss with the class the merits of humor, or make this a research project with older students. Discuss too the importance of giving "verbal warm fuzzies" to others. Have students practise doing this in small groups. Remind students to keep whatever they say specific. For example, say, *He is a good listener when I …* as opposed to *He is nice.*

4. Begin with a class assignment. Each student is expected to come to school the next day with a joke or amusing saying written on the back of "funny money" and to hang it on the money tree. There must be a name on each bill.

5. From then on, "funny money" may be taken from the box and used appropriately whenever a student "sees a need" (as demonstrated in **Tiny True Tale**). Assure students that they don't have to limit themselves to jokes. Any worthwhile, *positive* statement, such as *Thanks for helping me with my assignment,* is good too. Be sure to monitor that it isn't always the same students receiving messages. Invite students to read the backs of the "funny money" at appropriate times such as recess, or when work is completed.

6. You will need to "clear the tree" at various times. When you do this, be sure to give the bills to those whose names appear on them.

Quick Check: The Money Tree

- Is my tree sturdy enough to handle what's required of it? (If the branches are thin and brittle, they may break.)
- Do I have enough "funny money" bills in the box? (You will need to keep refilling the box.)

Steps for Students

1. Students think of something amusing, like a joke, or something that will make someone else smile or feel good. Occasionally, it is a good idea for them to draw names randomly so that every student will have a bill on the tree.

2. Each student neatly prints the chosen person's name on the back of a "funny money" bill, prints the message, and then signs it.

3. Students hang their messages on the money tree with opened paper clips and tell the recipients that they have done so.

Dealing with Diversities

Linguistic: Since the messages they will write will be read by all, encourage them to write as much as possible in both their first languages and English. Allow them to take "funny money" bills home, or provide a few minutes of time with an interpreter or someone who can translate.

Intellectual: If necessary, help these students to think in "specifics." Read their bills with them before they hang them so that they don't write anything that may cause them embarrassment.

Motivational and Behavioral: Invite these students to be the scribes for any students with physical diversities or students who need a little help with printing or spelling.

Gifted: These students may do the early research about the importance of humor and share it with the class. Similarly, they can be invited to find a bank of jokes, amusing quotes, and sayings that can serve as a resource for others wanting to write for a particular person, but looking for ideas about what to say.

Dealing with Developmental Levels

Kindergarten to Grade 3: The teacher will need to brainstorm and discuss with these children ways to express positive thoughts to others. As a class, they may make lists of appropriate thoughts, from which students can draw when they want to. Other than benefiting from help with spelling and formulation of thoughts, these students can handle this project beautifully on their own.

Grades 4 to 9: In some cases, you may have to limit the number of bills each student is allowed to hang per day as a few prolific writers will have the tree swamped very quickly. Limiting the number of bills on the tree to two received by the same student will keep the tree manageable.

Making Curriculum Connections and More

Language Arts: The money tree could inspire the making of posters and writing of songs to familiar words. For example, using the tune to "You Are My Sunshine," a student might get something like this:

> *Our money tree is so filled with humor.*
> *It makes us smile when we're feeling blue.*
> *So, if you're sad now, upset, or angry,*
> *You can read the money too.*

Students could also research humor, write humorous anecdotes and stories, and journal feelings associated with the giving and receiving of written "warm fuzzies."

Health: As extensions, the class could discuss the importance of showing respect, appreciation, and support for others, practise ways to do just that, or learn about the role that humor plays in health and identify other constructive ways to maintain good health, such as exercise.

Social Studies: Interested students could research people throughout the ages whose job was to make others laugh (e.g., court jesters and Aboriginal tribe pranksters). They could also research money and different forms of barter or trade.

Marvelous Masks of Many Colors

To be or not to be ...

What This Project Addresses

- personal identity
- creativity and perseverance
- problem solving: application of familiar techniques to unfamiliar situations
- planning and creating; synthesizing ideas
- curriculum connections: Language Arts, Health, Social Studies

Project Overview

Masks never cease to interest children. This project encourages them to experiment with different inner feelings and ideas of self and to try to represent these on a mask. It is wonderfully creative and, at times, cathartic.

Basically, the students are invited to collect materials that they will use to decorate personal masks and then let go. The results are often surprising and always interesting. It is important for you, the teacher, to have on hand a variety of materials to supplement what the students bring, but these need not be expensive or difficult to obtain.

Although there are many involved and creative ways to make masks, the fastest, cleanest, and easiest way is to begin with the small eye masks that show up at Halloween or can be purchased inexpensively the rest of the year at craft stores, dollar stores, or even floral warehouses.

TINY TRUE TALE

Margaret was from England and was used to being teased about her very obvious accent. When the "Marvelous Masks" project was introduced, she shared with the class two very ornate and old-looking English masks: one with sequins, feathers, and a long handle; the other, a big beaked thing. Apparently, her parents were collectors of such masks, and no doubt the ones she had brought to school were extremely valuable. Naturally, the other children were amazed, and Margaret was the instant centre of attention. The teacher worried that when the mask project was over, Margaret's unpopularity would resume. She was wrong. For whatever reason, Margaret had taken on a new persona in the eyes of her peers, especially since it seemed she had no shortage of ideas for the masks that the others were making. The teacher deemed the project successful in more ways than one.

Materials

- one mask for each child
- clear tape, staplers, or possibly children's clear glue
- paints (either poster or water color), felt pens, and oil pastel crayons
- odds and ends, such as feathers, bits of cloth, buttons, broken jewellery, ribbon, colored or sparkly pipe cleaners, artificial flowers, sequins, and sparkle dust (ask for donations from peers)

- magazines and scissors for collage effects
- a couple of real masks or pictures of masks

Steps for Teachers

1. Collect the necessary materials ahead of time.
2. Make a "half" mask. By that I mean, decorate one-half of an eye mask so students can see what the before and after would look like. This will be a model for them.
3. Discuss how masks should show something about the wearer. For example, you wouldn't put a flower on your mask if you didn't like flowers. Your half mask should clearly show something about you.
4. Discuss the various ways to stick things to the masks. Demonstrate.
5. Brainstorm together for ideas of what masks might look like and what sorts of things can be used to decorate them.

Quick Check: Marvelous Masks of Many Colors

- Am I prepared for frustration when glue won't hold? In other words, do I have tape and staplers available?
- Do the students have at least basic ideas of what they want to do with or on their masks before they begin?

Steps for Students

1. Students think of what they would like to put on their masks and collect items from home.
2. Students may want to sketch what they hope their finished masks will look like. They will get new ideas as they work.
3. Students need to remember that drawing, coloring, or gluing on the mask is not the same as on paper. They will need to experiment.
4. It is wise for students to start slowly, adding color first (if they want color), then adding other things.

Dealing with Diversities

Cultural: Often these children have more experience with masks than do the dominant culture students. They may be able to offer suggestions and help others.

Linguistic: It takes little language ability to understand this project, so they will be fine. Good suggestions are for these students to add words related to the mask making to their personal dictionaries and also to share their first language's word for mask with the rest of the class.

Physical: Depending on the challenge, some of these students will not be able to manage the mask making without a helper. Arranging to "borrow" an older student for the duration is one way to deal with this. The challenged student can give the directions and watch his or her mask take shape.

Gifted: Challenge these students to make their masks represent either their own heritages or that of some culture they admire, while at the same time, putting something of themselves on the mask. In addition, invite them to research and

Bring to class a couple of masks. If you can get your hands on some authentic cultural masks, that's great, but Halloween or wooden masks will work too. The more varied the masks you share with students, the more creative their own masks will be. You might also show pictures of masks. Your librarian will help here. Next, ask, *Who has ever worn a mask? When? Why?* Questions can lead to discussions about masks in general, and any children from another country or culture may be able to add insights into how they use masks.

write about the metaphorical "hiding behind masks"—why and how people do that—always keeping in mind that you do not want to pile extra work on these students, but to give them the option of these pursuits in place of some other task with which they are already familiar.

Dealing with Developmental Levels

Kindergarten to Grade 3: Due to the unfamiliarity with working on a curved surface, young children do better with just painting or coloring the white eye masks, then attaching one or two simple items with staplers. Another suggestion is to let them draw and color pictures to cut out and glue to the mask, then fix the pictures with white glue and leave the masks overnight.

Grades 4 to 9: The more brainstorming for decorating ideas before the decorating begins, the more creative the masks will be.

Making Curriculum Connections and More

Language Arts: Students may write stories based on the wearing of a mask, research literature to find characters who wore masks, and write poems about the completed masks. Other options include brainstorming for lists of adjectives for describing the masks and finding out how to say "mask" in as many languages as possible and creating a wall chart with this information.

Health: "Marvelous Masks of Many Colors" provides an opportunity to discuss how people hide behind masks metaphorically and what can be done to help them. Students could also write about themselves in terms of what parts of self were represented by their masks.

Social Studies: Extensions include researching masks in history; in other cultures around the world, especially those represented in the class; and in Canadian cultures, such as the West Coast Salish tribes or Inuit. Students could also compile charts of ways masks are used by different cultures.

Innovative Instruments

If music be the food of love, play on ...

What This Project Addresses

- explicit techniques to problem solve
- inventiveness and open-mindedness
- confidence in ability to present
- rhythm and music
- curriculum connections: Language Arts, Social Studies, Music, Art

Project Overview

We live in a noisy world. In addition to the myriad noises of existence, we are daily bombarded with music, rhythm, tunes, and lyrics. Children, fortunately, love rhythmic activities and music, so as teachers we should capitalize on this knowledge and build at least some of our teaching strategies based on it. "Innovative Instruments" is such a project.

Students, in groups of your choosing, are invited to create rhythm instruments from everyday items. This may seem like a daunting task, but the students are amazing. Then, once their instruments are finished, they can form mini-bands and "make music" either by keeping the rhythm to a tune with a strong beat, such as the "William Tell Overture" or the *Pink Panther* theme, or by creating words (usually hip-hop or chants) to accompany their "music."

In addition "Innovative Instruments" opens the door for much exciting follow-up learning dealing with music and bands, favorite musicians, and more.

TINY TRUE TALE

"I'm not making any stupid pretend instrument," Shawn complained. "I play a real guitar."

"Would you like to bring it to school?" the teacher asked.

"Maybe. But I'm not making any dumb thing."

"OK. But perhaps with your knowledge of guitars, you could help the rest of your group figure out what to do." The teacher was a bit concerned because Shawn was not known for his cooperative group activities.

Shawn shrugged and slumped off to where his group was brainstorming ideas. Soon the teacher noticed that Shawn had assumed leadership of the group and was drawing things on paper while the others watched with interest.

As it turned out, every member of Shawn's group created a stringed instrument using various sizes of elastic bands and shapes of cardboard. Their combined sound was amazing. Shawn never did make an instrument, but he was instrumental in the creation of the others' instruments. And when it came time to present, Shawn did bring his guitar to school to supplement his group's instruments—they provided the best presentation of all.

Materials

- any empty circular containers such as toilet paper rolls, throw-away plastic containers, cans, and jars
- an assortment of heavy cardboard pieces, which can be prepared by students cutting up boxes ahead of time
- an assortment of rubber bands some of them at least 1 cm wide in as many lengths as possible
- a wax paper roll
- a bag of gravel or small marbles
- tape and string
- bells, as in Christmas bells that you can buy in bulk at craft or dollar stores

Although students could gather these items themselves, it's good to have some on hand.

Plan to introduce this project by having students listen to a couple of pieces of music such as the two mentioned above. Let students keep the rhythm in any way they want to. Then open a discussion about bands, music, and rhythm. Ask, *Who plays a musical instrument?* or *Wouldn't it be fun to have our own bands?* Share pictures of musical instruments or if possible, bring an instrument to class; invite groups to brainstorm for ideas about creating their own "instruments." Think of all the Application skills they are using!

Steps for Teachers

1. Gather as many of the supplies as possible, as well as pictures of musical instruments.
2. Select a couple of pieces of music, considering the ages and tastes of the students.
3. Discuss the project and brainstorm as a whole class the sorts of things that might create sound, for example:
   - wax paper or packing tape pulled tightly over any empty circular object = drum
   - pebbles in empty container = castanets
   - bells attached to cardboard = tambourines
   - any hard-side items hit together = cymbals
   - elastics stretched over cardboard = guitars
   - sticks hit together = rhythm sticks
4. Put students in groups and allow a first meeting for discussion and planning and then a second meeting a couple of days later for creating the instruments with the supplies they have brought. Check regularly to see if they have necessary supplies.

Quick Check: Innovative Instruments

- Do the students have the concept—are they working toward a unified goal?
- Do I have a big enough supply of elastic bands?

Steps for Students

1. Once the teacher has introduced the project, students brainstorm for all the ways to make instruments, keeping a running record. They meet in groups and sketch ideas.
2. Over a few days, students collect and bring to school all the supplies they can find. They create their instruments "as a group"—helping one another—and decorating their instruments in any way they want to.
3. In their groups, students practise keeping rhythm with their new instruments and name their bands.
4. They perform as groups.

Dealing with Diversities

Cultural: These students, especially if they are First Nations children, may have many wonderful ideas for making drums, shakers, and more. This is a great opportunity to celebrate the diversity within the class and give students from divergent cultures a chance to be centre stage, so to speak.

Linguistic: The group work will be beneficial to these students, but be sure they understand the directions before they go to their groups.

Dealing with Developmental Levels

Kindergarten to Grade 3: You will need to demonstrate to the whole class a few methods of creating drums, for instance, by tightly attaching a circle of wax paper to the top of a toilet paper centre, using an elastic band, or guitars, by putting elastic bands around different sizes of cardboard to make the bands tight. Once they see a few demonstrations, students will be creative and find new ways.

Grades 4 to 9: Encourage as much variety within each group as possible. Promote the "band" concept—all working together to create one sound.

Making Curriculum Connections and More

For a wide variety of ideas for using music in the diverse classroom, refer to Appendix G, Tune Time.

3 Projects That Emphasize Analysis

Projects emphasizing Analysis involve all of the previously mentioned levels of thinking. Students break down material into component parts in order to better understand, identify, and illustrate the relationships among variables and elements.

Student success in this level of thinking is often measured by writings that clarify relationships such as cause and effect or comparison and contrast, describe patterns, or provide evidence or support for beliefs and conclusions. Questions beginning with *why* and *how* predominate here.

The projects described in this chapter move more deeply into Analysis as students look for reasons and explanations, identify motives and causes, and find evidence to support generalizations. In these projects, students learn more about themselves by scrutinizing themselves and others; they also learn more about projects by exploring their parts, then undertaking similar, but novel schemes on their own.

The following summarizes the main Analysis skills used in each project in this chapter.

Mirror Image Collages: Students will examine and do research on themselves, then will limit, prioritize, and illustrate pertinent points on self collages created within mirror frames.

"Iam Flip" Charts: As in "Mirror Image Collages," students will begin with self-examination and discovery, then will differentiate, prioritize, conclude, and outline pertinent facts on a flip chart in a pre-selected sequence.

Amazing Compilation Person: Students will question and debate in small groups, then limit, correlate, and illustrate specific positive characteristics of the group on a huge person outline.

Treasure Map: Students will research and relate to maps and treasure maps, then debate, refute, and defend ideas in order to create an innovative treasure map.

Whose Shoes? Footprints Poster: Students will research, classify, and examine the characteristics of a significant other; they will then compare, contrast, and relate the findings to themselves to establish reasons for their personal traits.

Cultural Calendars: Students will differentiate, discriminate, and research special celebrations, especially those relevant to students in the class. Then they will outline and illustrate these on calendars.

Tell Me a Story: Students will relate to storytelling; they will distinguish the characteristics of effective storytelling and will debate and defend their opinions before telling stories themselves.

Mirror Image Collages

Mislike me not for my complexion.

What This Project Addresses

- self-image and self-concept (sense of pride)
- cultural, ethnic heritage
- personal strengths
- communication and organization
- curriculum connections: Language Arts, Health, Social Studies, Art

Note: This project makes a good prerequisite for "Iam Flip" Charts which follows.

Project Overview

Mirror, mirror on the wall … What a familiar phrase that is, and it is one that will help us to help students learn more about themselves. When considering who and what they are, children too often see only what a mirror reflects; they don't realize just how multi-faceted they are. "Mirror Image" requires them to take a close look at themselves and in so doing, to take pride in their different backgrounds and individual strengths. It is a great self-awareness activity, and especially when there is a diverse population in a classroom, it helps everyone to get to know and appreciate everyone else a little better.

The idea is for students to find out as much as possible about themselves from the point of view of significant others and then to create framed personal collages that represent them. They begin by interviewing others, using a questionnaire with relatives and friends. Next, in small groups, they discuss the positive points of their peers. In these ways, students learn more about themselves. This information is then categorized and shown on a personal collage that is "inside a border to indicate a mirror." (See Figure 14.) Students can choose any way they want to present themselves, such as drawing, adding magazine pictures or real photographs, or writing phrases, poems, and descriptive words to their compilation collages.

TINY TRUE TALE

Tatu was a quiet, shy girl who had recently come to the Grade 2 class from Tanzania. She kept to herself and after a few unreciprocated attempts to include her in their activities, the rest of the children left her alone.

Then the class became involved in the "Mirror Image" project. The teacher encouraged the children to use personal ideas, based on what they could find out about their divergent backgrounds, and create the most colorful, detailed collages about themselves that they could.

Tatu's collage was amazing. She had not only filled the mirror with images, but also with short excerpts of a Swahili song and a few interesting and appropriate words, such as nikuone, *meaning let me see you.*

The other students were so entranced with Tatu's mirror collage that a barrage of questions followed, and it wasn't long until Tatu was a part of the group.

The collage appears within a foil-covered frame.

Figure 14

Either read or tell the Snow White fairy tale, with emphasis on the "mirror, mirror on the wall …" section. (Don't miss this great opportunity to point out that the stepmother is *stereotypical*, with the negative connotation attached to that. Many students will have excellent stepmothers, so it's important to take this teaching moment.)

Another good way to introduce this project is to have students sit facing a partner and try to copy each other's movements exactly, without making eye contact. Let them take turns "leading."

Be sure to discuss the fact that mirrors, although exact duplicates, are reversed images, and therefore not totally true.

Materials

- heavy paper for collage backs and mirror frames
- aluminium foil
- scissors and glue
- magazines
- coloring materials such as crayons, pencil crayons, markers, or oil pastels
- small mirrors (optional)
- class set of All about Me surveys

Steps for Teachers

1. Either have the frames prepared ahead of time (use that aide or peer helper), or plan to make the frames with students before beginning the rest of the project. If possible, purchase a small, pocket-size mirror for each student. Otherwise, arrange to have a couple of bigger mirrors in the room for the project. Photocopy the All about Me surveys.
2. You may wish to make a mirror image collage of yourself as a demonstration model. Although this will take a bit of time, remember that you can reuse this project with any grade for many years to come.
3. A good idea is to have a class discussion about specific positive ways to describe others. Ideas will likely include personality traits, athletic or artistic strengths, and a willingness to help others. This will help the students when they get into groups for "positive points discussions."
4. After you introduce the project, pass out mirrors, ask students to take a quick look at themselves, and then have them sketch themselves on blank paper. Collect the sketches and mirrors for later.
5. Break students into groups for further discussion before they begin individual work.
6. Once they have completed their first "Mirror Image" activities, give the mirrors back and have them repeat the sketching, asking if they see themselves any differently now. (Usually they do; if they don't, that's OK. The point is, they *know* more about themselves by now.)
7. Compare the before-and-after sketches.
8. Present the mirror image collages by wall mounting or sharing in groups.

Quick Check: Mirror Image Collages

- Have all students managed to get at least some of their surveys completed before they begin creating their mirror images?

Steps for Students

1. Students make frames by cutting out the inside of a piece of heavy paper or get them from the teacher. (Cutting through one corner to get to the middle is a good way to start.) Students cover their frames with foil.
2. Students look at their faces in the mirror provided for about 60 seconds. Then they put the mirror down and draw quick pictures of themselves, perhaps in cartoon style. They save the pictures.
3. Taking their All about Me surveys around to friends and family, they fill in as much of the first part as possible.

4. In small groups chosen by the teacher, students take turns talking about each person, listing as many positive traits that they see in a person as they can. These are "positive points discussions." Afterwards, they fill in the second part of the survey themselves.

5. Students begin collecting pictures, as well as odds and ends (e.g., pieces of cloth, such as a small piece of tartan). Students may collect special poems, sayings, words, or whatever will tell about them, their backgrounds, their history, and their families. They can draw or write on their pages too.

6. Students glue all their collections to pieces of paper and fasten the frames over them. Now they have their very own mirror images.

7. Finally, now that students have learned more about themselves, they look in the mirror again and sketch themselves a second time. They then look at the first sketches they drew and consider how their faces may have changed and what they have learned about themselves.

Dealing with Diversities

Cultural: Since this project truly celebrates diversity, encourage all students, but especially those from the non-dominant culture, to include pictures specific to their heritage.

Linguistic: Use an interpreter if necessary so as to stress the importance of using items specific to the first language and ethnic background.

Physical: Provide whatever assistance is necessary to allow these students to complete their mirror images too, but encourage them to think "outside" their disabilities or limitations. (In one instance, a girl in a wheelchair wanted a picture of herself as a ballerina because "in my mind that's who I am.")

Gifted: Encourage these students to "think metaphorically" and include more abstract representations, such as quotes from readings that they feel pertain to them and idioms, on their collages.

Dealing with Developmental Levels

Kindergarten to Grade 3: It is a good idea to have the frames pre-made for these students as making them takes unnecessary time away from the actual project. Also, a letter to parents explaining the project will ensure better participation on their part.

Grades 4 to 9: These students don't need much encouragement. They really take off on their own.

Making Curriculum Connections and More

Language Arts: Among many options are discussing and writing about how we learn about ourselves and benefit from feedback from others; reflecting on what students knew about themselves before and after completion of the project and creating suitable graphic organizers to show this; and writing autobiographical descriptions of self after finishing the collages.

Health: Students show appreciation and respect for others in group discussions using the "centre of the circle" technique. In groups of four or five, students take turns sitting in the centre, holding their mirror images. The person in the centre does not talk; the others provide positive feedback about the mirror as well as about the person showing it. Usually five minutes per person is sufficient. Students then write about their feelings in their journals.

Social Studies: When put in the light of Social Studies, "Mirror Image Collages" helps develop an awareness and appreciation of diversities. In a teacher-led discussion, diversities between students, which will be obvious when comparing the various mirrors, can be pointed out in a positive manner. Then the discussion can move specifically to any culture being studied at that time.

All about Me

Please help me to learn more about myself by completing or answering as many of these questions as you can.

Part 1

1. What was my favorite food as a baby? _____
2. What was the first word I said? In what language? _____
3. What color of hair did I have when I was born? _____
4. When you first saw me, what was your impression of me? _____
5. What was my favorite toy as a baby? _____
6. What made me angry when I was little? _____
7. Did I do anything that made you laugh? What? _____
8. How many living relatives do I have? _____
9. Where do they live? _____
10. Describe the place where I was born. _____

Part 2

1. My favorite color is _____
2. My favorite food is _____
3. My favorite song/music is _____
4. In my spare time, I like to _____
5. When I choose a friend, I look for _____
6. The thing that really makes me mad is _____
7. When I grow up, I want to be _____
8. When I grow up, I want to look like _____
9. When I grow up, a place I'd like to visit is _____
10. I am good at _____
11. My best physical feature is _____
12. My best personality trait is _____

"Iam Flip" Charts

I am constant as the Northern star.

Thanks to the students in the 2005 graduating class of the Grande Prairie Teacher Education North (TEN) program for this idea.

What This Project Addresses

• sequence and organization
• self-awareness: understanding of self
• surprise, anticipation, and prediction
• essential communication
• curriculum connections: Language Arts, Health

Note: This project follows "Mirror Image Collages" nicely.

Project Overview

Guessing games are an integral part of childhood. Consider the infamous knock-knock jokes. Children love to guess, especially when they can guess "right." In addition, they like to learn about one another, and they love surprises. "Iam Flip" Charts meets all of these criteria, and is easy to facilitate. ("Iam," pronounced just as it sounds, was coined by a Grade 5 class when they participated in the project.)

If students have already done "Mirror Image Collages," they will have the necessary information from which to create their "Iam Flips" (I-am-Flip-Charts). If not, then use the All about Me survey first, so that they have a good amount of personal information from which to work.

The idea is that students look at the posted flip charts to try to determine who each chart is about, before getting to the final, name-revealing page. (See Figure 15.)

Flip charts can be any size, but probably the easiest is the regular 8 by 11 paper cut in half lengthwise. The backing needs to be firm. The thin cardboard from packing cases is perfect, but any card-weight paper will do.

The students prepare as many pages as they want to, each page featuring a different piece of information about themselves, but without revealing their names. The flip pages are then attached with staples, tape, rings, ribbon ties or even coils, in such a way that the first pages to be seen give way the least information about the person. For example, page 1 might simply show a picture of a horse (the student enjoys horseback riding), the second might have a poem about happiness (from the survey the student realizes others see her as always being happy), and so on. When attaching these pages together, consider that they will be "flipped," or turned, frequently. The easiest pages for little hands to flip are those attached by ordinary loose-leaf rings.

"Iam Flips" can be posted on walls for display. They are wonderful when parents are visiting and can try to find the "Iam Flips" of their own children.

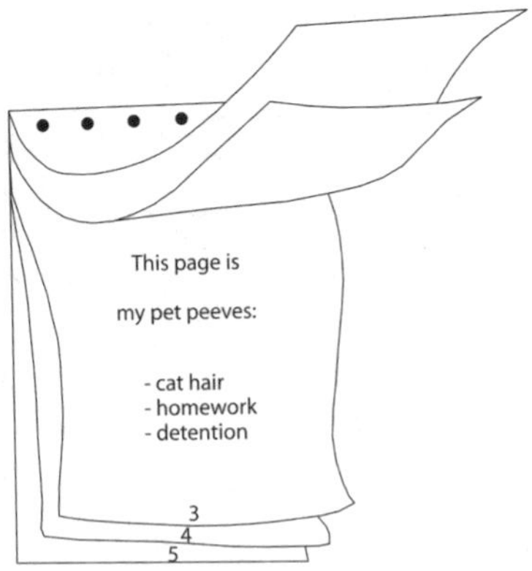

This page is
my pet peeves:

- cat hair
- homework
- detention

3
4
5

The name is not revealed until the last page.

Figure 15

"I know that's yours, Billy, because you are the best ball player in the room!"

"Nope! Not mine!"

"Yeah, but look at the next page—a picture of a bike and some boxing gloves. You have boxing gloves, don't you?"

"Yep! But it's not mine."

"And the fishing rod. I know you go fishing at the creek. I've gone there with you. It's got to be yours."

"Not! Why don't you look at the last page and find out?"

The young man, Scott, quickly flipped the pages to the last one and saw the smiling face of Jennifer, another classmate, glued there. He looked shocked. Jennifer looked extremely pleased.

"What did you learn from that, Scott?" the teacher asked calmly.

Pose the question "Do others know the real you?" Discuss with the class how people often show to others only what they want to. Suggest that this project will be like a guessing game where others get a peek into parts of them they might not know about. Reassure students that they need not reveal anything they don't want to. The students could spend a few minutes making guesses about one another with non-threatening questions such as *Who in the class had a birthday last week? Who do you think will be at least six feet tall when he finishes growing?*

Materials

- heavy paper or card for backing
- lots of smaller cut pages, about 7–10 sheets per student
- whatever book "fastening" materials you choose (coils, rings, tape …)
- All about Me surveys (if not already done)
- magazines
- scissors, glue

Steps for Teachers

1. Explain the purpose: the flip charts reveal only one page at a time and should not immediately give away who the "Iam Flip" is about; succeeding pages will provide more and more hints, and the last page will have the name or photo of the person.
2. If possible, show an example of some sort of flip chart as a demonstration.

Quick Check: "Iam Flip" Charts

- Do students understand the basic premise of gradually giving more and more details as to whom the "Iam Flip" is about?

Steps for Students

1. Students gather information about themselves from friends, parents, and relatives. Using the All about Me survey could be helpful.
2. They find pictures in magazines, draw pictures, or write appropriate phrases, sentences, poems, or whatever they choose, to tell *something* about themselves.
3. Using at least seven pages each, students put something about themselves on each page. They may use as many pages as they want as long as each page reveals something about them. Here is an example:
   a. Page 1: a picture of something the student did, said, or liked as a baby
   b. Page 2: a picture of the student's favorite food, on a background of a favorite color

    c. Page 3: a piece of writing (poem, short story, paragraph) that tells something about the student

    d. Page 4: something that shows what the student wants to do or be as an adult

    e. Page 5: something from the student's cultural, ethnic, or religious background (carefully presented as this could give him or her away)

    f. Page 6: something others don't know about the student, but the student would like them to know

    g. Page 7: a "give-away" piece of information *or* photograph

4. Students attach all their pages together at the top, to allow others to "flip" through them and see who they are about.

Dealing with Diversities

Cultural and Religious: Invite these students to use symbolism or illustrations depicting their diversities, but to save these for the latter pages so as not to give "Iam Flip" identities away too quickly.

Linguistic: This activity reinforces beginning English vocabulary well, but encourage ESL students to write in their first languages too, especially on the later pages so as not to give away their identities too quickly. In this way you are celebrating their languages and giving the English-speaking students exposure to them.

Intellectual: These students may need assistance in organizing their flips, so as to not be overly obvious on the first few pages.

Motivational and Behavioral: Usually these students really enjoy this project, but keep an eye on what they are putting on each page so as to avoid unfortunate surprises. (I recall one student who glued a magazine picture of a homicide being committed to one of his pages.)

Gifted: Encourage subtlety, illusions, and metaphorical statements.

Dealing with Developmental Levels

Kindergarten to Grade 3: Do one page at a time with younger students, so as to avoid confusion, and specify what should go on each page.

Grades 4 to 9: Encourage creativity and subtlety.

Making Curriculum Connections and More

Language Arts: Follow-ups include writing letters of appreciation to those who completed the survey questionnaires, writing biographical descriptions of classmates based on what is in the "Iam Flips," and writing, telling, or reading mystery-type stories where the reader has to make guesses based on clues.

Health: Through discussion about the "Iam Flips," students may develop appreciation for individual differences and journal or chart their findings.

Amazing Compilation Person

To be or not to be—that is the question.

Thanks to the students in the 2005 graduating class of the Grande Prairie Teacher Education North (TEN) program for this idea.

What This Project Addresses

- cooperation
- personal importance
- creativity
- peer support
- awareness of linguistic idioms
- mutual conclusions arrived at through discussion, questioning, and debating
- curriculum connections: Language Arts, Health, Social Studies, Science, Mathematics, Physical Education, Art

Project Overview

How many times have you wished you could be several people at the same time? A "compilation" of various persons. For teachers, I think this is a common wish. The way we "make the wish come true" is, more often than not, to solicit the help of peers. Consequently, helping your students understand the value of "putting our strengths together" should be relatively easy. Plan to introduce the term *compilation*—a whole lot of different things in one place—no matter how young your students are because they will enjoy learning a new, interesting word, and point out how compilation can work for them.

Often, it is difficult for students to work cooperatively in groups, and yet all evidence points to the fact that the best learning comes from peers. "Amazing Compilation Person" directly addresses this issue by enabling students to examine the positive traits of all group members and put them together to create a new compilation person. (Be sure to provide the definition of the word.) Students become excited to see how many excellent traits their new person—actually the group—displays. This ends up being a visual display that reminds all of us that we are not alone and that we gain strength from others.

Basically, students think together of the two or three *best* traits of each individual in the group, and write or illustrate them *inside* a large outline of a gingerbread figure without features other than amorphous arms, legs, and head. (See Figure 16.) If students get hung up on a particular trait, such as being friendly, offer other suggestions and encourage thinking along the lines of "What else can _____ do?"

I like the way this project includes all children, even if they can't speak a word of the dominant language, because peers will think of their best traits for them. In addition, the final, posted projects are colorful reminders of all the positive traits within the class.

Gingerbread "Compilation Person"

This figure can be enlarged.

Joe was a Grade 6 Métis boy who seldom spoke and stayed alone on the playground. He usually had a scowl on his face and his head down. The other students avoided him. They seemed to be almost afraid of him. During the "Compilation Person" project one popular girl, Anne, seemed to take it upon herself to get all the others in the group to think of many positive traits that applied to Joe. They really got into it. After starting with "quiet" (no surprise there), they added words like "thoughtful, gentle, wise, strong, good at sports, good listener." Joe seemed really pleased. (I was thrilled.) I noticed that the group put more of Joe's good traits into the compilation person than they did of anyone else's. Their finished product was a work of art—and quite an amazing personality! But the best part was that the next day, Joe sat with Anne at recess.

Materials

- large, stiff chart paper, preferably Bristol board
- colored markers

Steps for Teachers

Ask students to list their good qualities on paper. Make the comment that it would be great if we could have *all* the good qualities of everyone in one person. Then you and the class are on your way!

1. Divide your class into heterogeneous groups of about five members each, being sure to have a good mixture of diversities in each group. Write the names of each group member on the back of the poster paper.
2. Discuss the word "compilation." With younger children, adaptations may be necessary (see **Dealing with Developmental Levels**).
3. Brainstorm for "positive" traits that people in general may have. It is important to move students away from vague, meaningless words like "nice" and "good" to more creative and descriptive words and phrases.
4. Draw a model of a gingerbread person on the board. (See Figure 16.) Explain the process and let the groups work.
5. Bring the whole class together at the end to discuss the completed characters. Summarize with talk about the importance of combining efforts, helping one another and so on. You can bring in pieces of folk wisdom, such as these idioms: *Two heads are better than one. United we stand, divided we fall. The more the merrier. Let's put our heads together. It takes two to tango.*

Quick Check: *Amazing Compilation Person*

- Is the poster paper stiff enough to deal with a lot of handling and many drawings or writings without tearing or wrinkling?
- Does each group have a large, workable, clearly marked outline of a gingerbread person?

Steps for Students

1. Students discuss in their groups the positive traits of each member in turn. They must think of as many *different* positive things about one another as possible.

2. Working with a drawn or outlined gingerbread person, students pick two or three of the best qualities of each person in the group and put them in the figure. They are free to use words, phrases, illustrations, or a combination of all.
3. Every group gives their amazing new person a name and prepares to share with the class.
4. The group-created figures are posted on a wall for all to see.

Dealing with Diversities

Cultural: Encourage students to realize that all of them are basically the same and have similar traits. Watch for stereotyping, such as all First Nations children are creative, even if it is *positive* stereotyping, and be prepared to deal with it, if necessary.

Linguistic: Once ESL students figure out what is going on (and they will, even without interpreters), allow them to change the positive traits awarded to them in English, to their first languages. List the traits in the compilation person in these languages. It may even be possible to write *every* trait in the compilation person in more than one language.

Motivational: Often, having these students "fill in" the traits with colored pen adds a dimension of interest for them.

Gifted: Encourage these students to be the "thesaurus users" in their groups and to find "better ways to describe" by using the thesaurus as well as their own knowledge.

Dealing with Developmental Levels

Kindergarten to Grade 3: It may be necessary for the teacher to draw the initial pencil outlines of the generic characters on the poster paper. It may also be necessary to assist students in the whole-group setting to think of all the possible positive traits people can have, before separating into groups. Encourage very young children to draw, rather than write, the traits.

Grades 4 to 9: Encourage students to look beyond surface characteristics. For example, ask: *What makes that person do so well in school? at sports? Why is that person always early to school? Why do kids like to hang around that person? What enables that person to work so quietly on his own?*

Making Curriculum Connections and More

Language Arts: Students may create spelling lists from words in the characters and perhaps work with a thesaurus properly. They could create stories about the adventures of the compilation people or write personal reflections using the "good traits" about themselves as indicated by peers.

Health: Students could build on the project by discussing the importance of positive actions and developing an awareness of individual strengths. They could also be encouraged to reflect in writing or through discussion how some of their positive personal traits have come from or been influenced by others.

Social Studies: Connections include researching successful groups in history and looking for news articles about groups that do good works, such as raising funds or offering support. Students could identify possible applications of what was learned, such as raising barns; holding bake sales and special events such as school fun fairs; making and maintaining nature trails; and building houses, such as for Habitat for Humanity.

Mathematics: There are several related concepts, such as combining (adding and multiplying), learning about parts and wholes, dividing large parts into composites, learning about fractions, and measuring distances around.

Science: Students could apply their understanding by learning how groups in nature function based on the strengths/weaknesses of individual members, and discussing how animals, such as wolves in packs, cooperate.

Physical Education: Taking part in cooperative games (e.g., working together to build a human pyramid), meeting team challenges where all members help one another to finish, and working as team members for any team sports parallel the values of the "Amazing Compilation Person" project.

Treasure Map

Ah but—to go we know not where …

What This Project Addresses

- creativity and imagination
- analysis, interpretation, and comprehension of maps and mapping
- exploration and discovery of text features that enhance understanding
- utilization of prior knowledge about maps and history
- curriculum connections: Language Arts, Health, Social Studies, Mathematics

Project Overview

I think there's a spirit of adventure in everyone, especially in teachers. Most certainly it's there in our students. And what greater adventure than finding a buried treasure? Perhaps creating a map of a hypothetical buried treasure can come close.

By using researching, interpreting, analysing, and organizing skills, students make their very own treasure maps. First, they create "antique paper," one piece per group. Then, as a group, students plan the map and come to a mutual decision as to exactly *what* the treasure is and *where* it will be found. One or two members are chosen to carefully plot out a treasure map on the antiqued paper. The fun (and inherent learning) is in the creation of the maps themselves, and the finished products never cease to amaze both students and teachers.

Once students are motivated to create their own maps, the teacher's job is simply to oversee. There is little to do but "let them learn," and few students do not want to be involved. The whole idea of finding buried treasure is appealing to them, as are images of pirates, deserted islands, and gold.

TINY TRUE TALE

"Can I make another map, Mr. Y?" Alicia asked. Mr. Y looked at her in amazement. Alicia was generally apathetic about most in-class activities, especially when they involved group work. In fact, he thought she had contributed very little to her group's "Treasure Map" project and was surprised she wanted to do one on her own.

"Of course. But you'll have to find the time on your own. I can't give you any more class time."

"That's OK as long as I can use the class stuff. This was a fun assignment. Next time I want to make my map go through the mountains where we camped last year. Maybe in caves or something. The one my group did was OK, but they all wanted to make an island map. My mountain map will be even better. You'll see."

He did see. Alicia's map was innovative, detailed, and creative. He also saw that before creating her map she had researched the mountainous area where she had camped with her family. Mr. Y was immediately convinced of the merits of this project and vowed to allow even more time for it next year.

Rice paper is perfect for this project, but it is expensive so you probably won't want to use it unless the finished products are to be featured in some very special manner. If you decide to use tea or coffee to darken the maps, be sure to experiment first. Remember that the maps need to be light enough to draw or write on.

Consulting the school librarian for stories about maps and treasures can be helpful.

Materials

- sheets of lightweight white paper, perhaps from a roll or designed for drawing—not newsprint
- soft lead pencils, especially the "fat" primer pencils; *waterproof* black felt pens; charcoal sticks (optional)
- strong, cold coffee (about 1 tsp instant coffee to a half cup of water), strong tea, *or* a watery mixture of brown tempera or powder paint
- old maps
- stories, books, and pictures about pirates and treasure maps
- paper towels

Steps for Teachers

1. Tap into students' innate sense of adventure by having the class share any stories about pirates, hidden treasures, or treasure maps. Another idea is to share a modern-day road map and find various routes. Once you have used your motivational material, talk about how treasure maps often have "false leads," traps, dead-ends, and other obstacles.
2. Examine some maps together. (This project is a great addendum to a Social Studies unit on mapping and geography, but it is not necessary to be pursuing that part of the curriculum.)
3. Prepare a small pail or bowl of strong black coffee or tea (or diluted brown poster paint) for submerging the paper, as well as a pail of clean water. The integrity of the paper must be destroyed a bit before putting in the stain, so wet and crumple it first. Submerge the paper for at least a few minutes, to allow it to take on a wonderful aged look. The length of time required for submersion will depend on the integrity of the paper as well as the strength of the "dye." Experiment. You will simply provide the bath; the students themselves will create the antiqued paper.
4. Group students heterogeneously, and provide each group with sketch and map paper.

Quick Check: Treasure Map

- Do I have an old towel or rag on hand in case of "tea spills"?
- Do the students all have a rough draft before they begin marking their map paper?

Steps for Students

1. Students wet the map paper and then carefully wrinkle it into a ball. They dip it in the "dye" bath and let it remain for about two minutes, or until they are satisfied with the color.
2. The paper is opened carefully. It will now be covered with many darker wrinkle lines. Students spread the paper out on a paper towel and allow it to dry completely.
3. In their groups of four or five, students discuss what kind of treasure their map will lead to and where in the world they will set their map.
4. Next, the groups determine what sort of obstacles will interfere with the finding of the treasure.

5. Students sketch their rough draft together, on plain paper, remembering to include lots of traps and obstacles along the way. They think of interesting ways to illustrate landforms, as well as things like trees, rocks, quicksand, waterfalls, and rivers. Each group will complete only one map.

6. The good map is plotted lightly on the antiqued map paper that students have created. As one member is plotting the map, another keeps a written record of the trip the "map holder(s)" will follow.

7. Students carefully go over the pencil lines with waterproof felt pen, and add as many interesting features, including a legend if they want to, as they can. If desired, they may add shading with charcoal, perhaps on mountains or in river beds.

8. The final step is to tear the edges of the map carefully, to give it a rough, well-worn look. (See Figure 17.)

Dealing with Diversities

Cultural: These students may have appropriate stories from their own backgrounds that they can be encouraged to share.

Linguistic: Little is needed as the students will quickly catch on to what is expected and be willing to help.

Motivational and Behavioral: Ask these students to assist with the "dye baths" for the map paper and with the final posting of the finished maps.

Gifted: Invite these students to research treasures that remain unfound and to share their findings with the class.

Dealing with Developmental Levels

Kindergarten to Grade 3: Even little hands love this project. However, it may be best for an adult to do all the "dye baths" and flattening (to avoid tearing), and perhaps to have an aide, volunteer, parent, or older student help the groups to get started.

Grades 4 to 9: The best part of this project is the many post-map activities in which these students can participate. See **Making Curriculum Connections and More.**

Making Curriculum Connections and More

Language Arts: This project lends itself to many types of writing:

- writing stories to accompany the maps, either about the persons who *hid* the treasures and made the maps, or the persons who *followed* the maps
- writing directions to a specific place in the community
- plotting routes to places using real maps and real places, and then writing accompanying directions
- writing journal entries from the point of view of the pirate who hid the treasure
- writing a script about treasure hunting and casting real movie stars for the parts, followed up by a drama presentation
- writing poems on antiqued paper about the feelings experienced while seeking a treasure or being shipwrecked on a deserted island

Note the ragged edges of the antique-looking map.

Figure 17

- making Wanted posters for the pirates who stole the buried treasure
- writing detailed descriptions of the treasures

Health: Comparing the hygiene habits of pirates to the habits we have today might be an interesting extension.

Social Studies: Students could follow up by researching and learning about real lost treasures, sunken ships, and riches; they could also locate directions (north, south, east, west) on maps.

Mathematics: There are aspects of measuring in the use of maps and legends for distances, and for discovery of angles.

Whose Shoes? Footprints Poster

I am my father's spirit ...

What This Project Addresses

- personal identity and heritage
- personality plus personal strengths, weaknesses, likes, and dislikes
- family and personal values
- independent research and work
- curriculum connections: Language Arts, Health, Social Studies

Project Overview

"You have your father's eyes." A common statement—one that points out an important truism. Individuals enjoy being associated with the positive traits of significant others, because it is a way to evaluate themselves and develop self-worth. We all like to feel special. We all need to be seen as individuals. Yet we take pleasure in being told we are "like so-and-so" especially when that so-and-so is someone we love and respect. "Whose Shoes?" encourages students to look closely at themselves and determine in "whose shoes" they walk. In other words, who do they most resemble and from whom have they most probably learned or acquired specific positive traits? Students are encouraged to find out *who* they are, and, as much as possible, *why* they are. In other words, they examine reasons for why they are the way they are, both physically and emotionally. (*My dad is tall; I am tall. My mom is shy; I am shy.*)

For some students, this is a wake-up activity; for others, it is a reaffirmation of what they already know, or perhaps even a denial of what they don't want to know. In any event, it is a worthwhile research into self, with a beautiful "Footprints poster" as the culminating element.

Basically, with the help of peers, students think of as many personal attributes associated with significant others as they can. They then put this information on footprints ("shoes") in a variety of individual ways. In the event that you have students, perhaps from foster homes or group homes, who may be unable to consider any relatives, assure them that they may choose whomever they want as models, perhaps teachers, mentors, older friends, and coaches.

Be sure to introduce "Whose Shoes?" as a celebration of self.

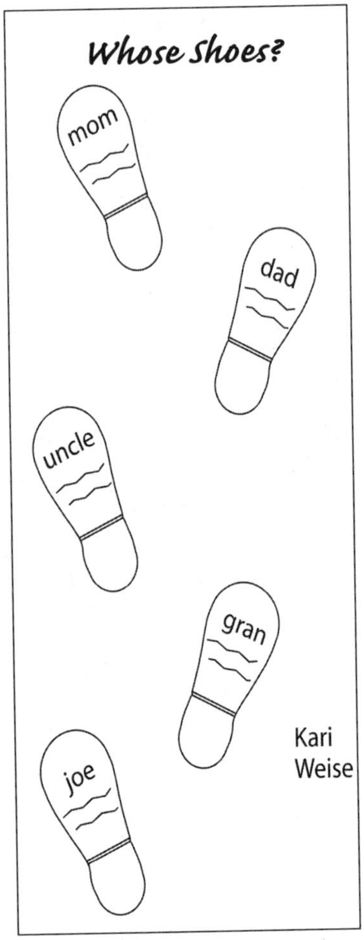

TINY TRUE TALE

"Why do you have only two footprints on your poster?" Molly, a small, very white skinned girl, asked Raji, a small, very not-so-white-skinned boy.

"Because I have only two grandparents and they have very big shoes. Why do you have so many footprints?"

"I have lots of nannas and aunties and cousins and ..."

"And do you take parts from all of them?"

Silence!

No more was said, but the next time the teacher saw Molly's poster, there were considerably fewer footprints than there had been before. Children learn so much from each other!

Whose Shoes?

mom

dad

uncle

gran

joe

Kari Weise

In answering the question "Whose Shoes?" students produce posters that are explorations of self.

Figure 18

Whose Shoes? Footprint

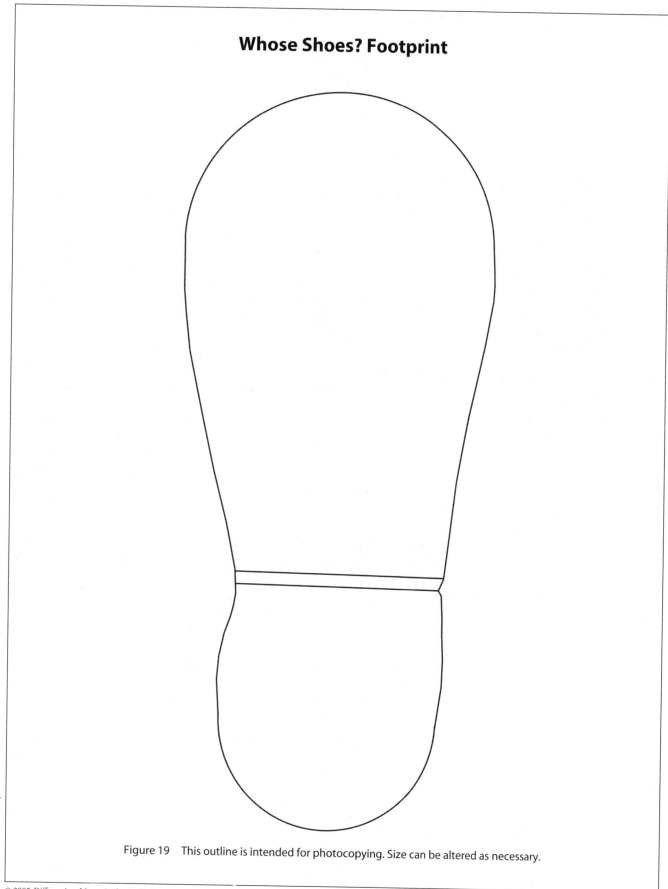

Figure 19   This outline is intended for photocopying. Size can be altered as necessary.

Materials

- colored heavy-weight poster paper larger than 8 by 11—large sheets of construction paper work well.
- footprints—outlines of "shoes"
- scissors and glue
- coloring materials

Be sure to prepare the shoes ahead of time by photocopying the master provided (Figure 19). You will need at least two per student.

Steps for Teachers

1. Prepare the footprints.
2. Locate any materials that will work as motivators for the project, including picture books, stories about "being like our parents or grandparents" and pictures of families of different nationalities.
3. Introduce the project and discuss the ways we learn from other people. Use the idea that we "walk in the shoes of others." You may wish to relate this back to the First Nations people who use the phrase "walk in his moccasins" and how it is not a good idea to judge a person until you have had similar experiences.
4. As a class, brainstorm for characteristics or preferences that might be due to association with someone else or physical traits that might be from a parent. For example, point out how hair and eye color are inherited physical traits, but an enjoyment of fishing might be a shared pleasure, an interest, learned from a grandparent. List some ideas on the board or on chart paper for later reference.
5. Explain that on each footprint the child writes the name of one person, plus whatever traits were gained or learned from that person. Be sure to note that traits may be physical or personality based, as well as representative of interests and abilities. (This may be a good time for a mini-lesson on the difference between physical and personality traits, if you have not done this previously.) Share one filled-in footprints poster relating to *yourself*. (See Figure 20 as an example.)
6. Remember to point out that although we may "walk in the shoes of others" and be affected by them, we still *choose* who we are and how we will act in certain situations.
7. Put students in small groups where they talk about ways they are like their parents/guardians or relatives. For example, a student may point out that another is a good reader who reads a lot, ask whether his mother also reads a lot, and tie the two facts together.
8. Display the completed "Whose Shoes?" posters with a brief description of their content: *So many people change us, when we walk in their shoes. They have so many qualities. From these traits we pick and choose.*

Establish a *need* for students to learn more about themselves. You may simply pose a question, "Why are you the way you are today?" Or, use this project as an introduction to a theme or Health unit about self, or as a follow-up to a relevant story. An excellent picture book that sets the scene for this type of thinking is *Two Pairs of Shoes* by Esther Sanderson. It works even with Grade 9 students. Other resources for establishing the correct mindset are *If You Could Wear My Sneakers*, a poetry book by Sheree Fitch in which each poem is written from the point of view of someone from a different diversity, and *Walk Two Moons* by Sharon Creech.

Quick Check: Whose Shoes? Footprints Poster

- Do I have enough footprints ready in advance?
- Are any students likely to need help identifying personal traits?

Steps for Students

1. In small groups, students think of one another's physical and personality traits, as well as particular interests and abilities. In other words, they share

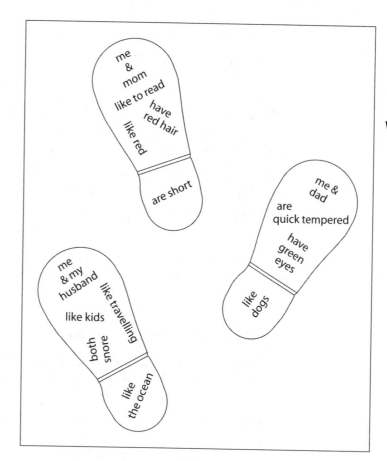

Figure 20

what they know about the people in their small group, keeping a list of what others say about them, if they can.

2. On their own, students then think of several people who have had a great influence on them—people in *whose shoes* they sometimes or always walk. They try to connect these people to things they know about themselves. For example, if someone is a good swimmer, is it because a parent is a good swimmer? Students may find that several of their traits, interests, and abilities can be associated with one person.

3. On practice paper, they write the names of this person or of several people, and list what they have gained from them. For example: My Mom—red hair, sense of humor, ability to sing, quick temper.

4. Once students have their lists completed, they print them neatly on *one* footprint each and then decorate the footprint in a way that reminds them of that special person. Each footprint used will compare the student to just one other person.

5. When students have several footprints completed, they may arrange them on the poster paper in whatever way they want. They can "make a path" (see Figures 18 and 20) or a collage. The poster represents in whose shoes they walk.

Dealing with Diversities

Cultural: Encourage these students to think of people who may be in countries far away, as well as those close at hand. If they want to alter the "shape" of the

93

footprints, to something more suitable to their cultures, encourage that. For example, I have seen First Nations children add decorations to the amorphous footprints to make them look more like moccasins, and a Chinese girl decorated the toes of her footprints with drawings that resembled oriental embroidery.

Linguistic: Just be sure these students understand the project and then encourage them to write on their footprints using their first languages, and, if they want, to include as many English words as possible.

Socio-economic: If immediate role models seem absent, be ready to suggest that students consider teachers, coaches, even peers.

Intellectual: If the concept seems too abstract, make specific, concrete suggestions or limit the task to obvious physical traits.

Gifted: Challenge these students to look deeply at their own personalities and find both similarities and differences between the people they select as their "shoes."

Dealing with Developmental Levels

Kindergarten to Grade 3: Having the footprints already cut out for them with lines on each foot facilitates printing. Also, making the footprints slightly bigger for ease of printing may be helpful.

Grades 4 to 9: Encourage alterations to the footprints to show different kinds of shoes. For example, if the "model" is a rancher who wears cowboy boots, how can the student make the footprint look more like a boot print? Also, encourage as much writing as possible on each footprint, as well as background decorations that fit the "model." For the rancher, the background might include a rope or a horse.

Making Curriculum Connections and More

Language Arts: Students could write letters to any of the models featured on the footprints, to thank them for their influence. They could orally share information from their posters with others in a small group. An interesting extension would be reading a story and hypothesizing about how or where the protagonist got his traits.

Health: The class could take the opportunity to discuss the importance of families, peers, and role models, as well as choices, or learn more about personalities, and positive or negative character traits. They might take this further by thinking of a personal skill or interest that they could share with someone else, such as a younger sibling or grandparent, in order to help that person develop an interest in, and enjoyment of, the activity.

Social Studies: Extensions might be learning how our ancestors were affected by their peers or studying First Nations cultures and their belief in the importance of elders.

Cultural Calendars

Let every man be master of his time.

What This Project Addresses

- cultural and religious diversity
- analysis of time frames
- appreciation, respect, and tolerance for others
- construction of accurate representations of information.
- gathering and connecting information so as to reach new conclusions
- curriculum connections: Language Arts, Health, Social Studies

Project Overview

Ever missed someone's birthday because you didn't have it marked on a readily visible calendar? As teachers, we have so many important work-related happenings throughout the year that missing a birthday is easy to do. But there are other important days we can easily miss too, perhaps more from ignorance than lack of remembering. These are the many days that are significant culturally or religiously.

With a diverse population in the classroom and community, teachers often find themselves caught off guard when a student announces an upcoming absence for a special day related to the child's culture or religion. Immediately, questions are raised by other students, curious to learn about their peers. The best way to deal with this situation is to prepare everyone ahead of time by making month-to-month page calendars that clearly show and illustrate as many special days as possible. It is usually a good idea to create the cultural calendars early in the school year so that they are available and visible for the entire term.

There are a couple of ways to handle the creation of the cultural calendars. Students can work from photocopies of the current year calendar (see Figure 21). For younger students (with smaller hands) you can enlarge the special days on a regular calendar, by using a little white-out and creating an increased size square, as on Figure 22. Or, a calendar can be made to look like a three-column chart giving the name of the celebration, date, and description of each event.

You will want to limit the special days marked on your calendars to those specifically celebrated by class members, their families, and you. Any attempt to include all cultural and religious celebrations would be overwhelming, and since many dates change from year to year, impossible. Send home a Special Days Family survey, such as the one included with this project, together with a letter. Once all the surveys have been returned, the class can begin the project.

Beyond the personal special celebrations that the class with mark on their calendars, you may want to include any school festivities or activities such as track and field events, concerts, and field trips. Doing so will make the calendars complete representations of the school year.

It is usually a good idea to create the calendars early in the school year. It will probably take two or three classes to locate all the dates on the calendars; then students could "decorate" the marked dates either on their own time, after work is completed, or in a class set aside for that purpose.

The finished calendars go home with students, but do keep one at school as an instant reminder for yourself.

If you get one or two excellent calendars (or a calendar that is a compilation of pages from different students), consider making copies and selling these in the school. This may be an excellent way to make a little money for other special projects.

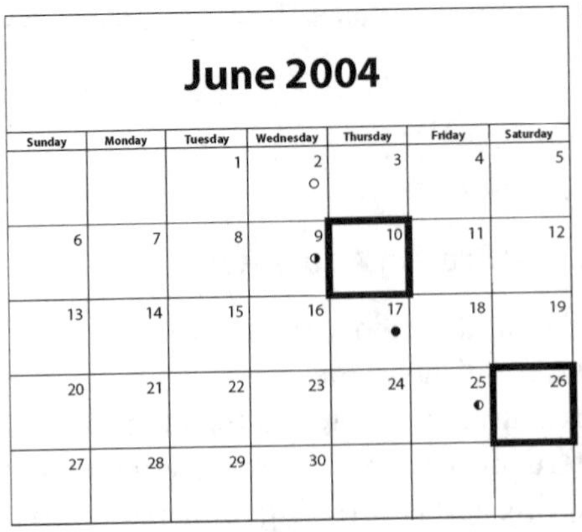

Figure 21

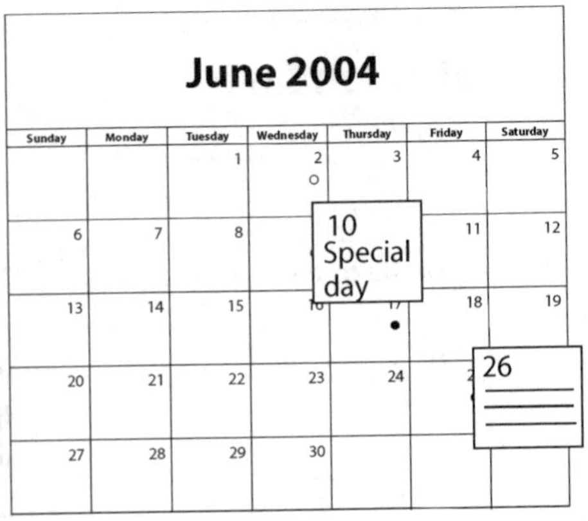

Figure 22

TINY TRUE TALE

*"Boy, I didn't know there were so many different holidays every month,"
a young lad remarked to his teacher.*

*"Yes," the teacher replied, pleased that the boy was so interested in all
the diversity they had discovered within their classroom.*

*"You know what?" The boy went on, eyes wide with assumed
innocence, "Don't you think it would be good if we celebrated all of
them—you know—to show that we like everyone equal? 'Cause just
having holidays on our days isn't fair."*

"But that would mean a holiday about every week," the teacher said.

"Yep!" the boy beamed.

Materials

- calendar pages for students
- pencils, pencil crayons, or fine-point felt pens
- erasers
- scissors, glue, magazines
- construction paper for calendar covers
- method of fastening pages: coiling is best but tying with string or ribbon works too
- Special Days Family Survey and letter, one per student

Steps for Teachers

Open a discussion about the many different ways people celebrate. Brainstorm in the class for special days. Point out that in addition to birthdays, there are many other important days too, and keeping track of them can be a problem. Discuss the importance of the calendars that students are going to make.

1. Decide how you want the students' finished calendars to look and make the necessary photocopies. If using a "current year" calendar, remember to allow enough room to write or draw on specific dates. You may wish to enlarge a regular-sized calendar so that the squares are easier for writing.

2. Using the returned and completed Special Days Family Surveys, decide ahead of time which special dates you will mark for each month. You will need to collate the information provided by students and their families. Although students from Grade 4 on can collate information in groups of three or four, it will be more time efficient for you or a volunteer to do this before your first time working on the calendars. The quickest way to accomplish this may be to have a blank page for each month, then list any special days, birthdays, school events, and so

on occurring in that month. With the class, you can then decide which dates to mark on the calendars. If you choose to have students collate, though, make each group responsible for determining the special days for one month.

3. Discuss diversity as related to special days, being sure to celebrate the wonderful variety within the classroom and community.

4. You may want to make an overhead of the first month and use it to demonstrate how to mark the first special day by writing or drawing *in* the appropriate square.

5. It may be appropriate to discuss *symbols* with students also, so that they can better illustrate specific dates. Students are more likely to use established symbols, such as eggs and candles, for familiar events. You might also broaden their knowledge of symbols. Invite students celebrating what may be less familiar special days to share any symbols specific to these celebrations. Not all special days need to be illustrated or symbolized, though; in some cases, just highlighting the date will be sufficient.

6. Collect pages that are "works-in-progress" and keep them until all months are finished; otherwise, you know what will happen to them. I found that keeping a different file folder for each month simplified matters when it came to putting the calendars together.

Quick Check: Cultural Calendars

- Do I want to complete the entire calendar at once, and if so, do I have enough calendar pages ready?
- Have I received information from all families of students in my class?
- Is the information collated, either by myself or by student groups?
- Are there any parents/guardians I would like to invite to speak to the class about particular celebrations?

Steps for Students

1. Students follow the teacher's example and mark the first special date. They begin by outlining the box with a colored pencil (see Figure 21) or by neatly printing the name and date of the special day on their page (Figure 22).

2. For each special day, students think of a *symbol* or small image and draw it in the square or after the date. If a symbol is not known for a particular day, the box can simply be colored, or students may ask the teacher or their peers for the necessary information. They try to keep their printing neat and their illustrations small.

3. Students make sure that their names are on the backs of all pages they do.

4. When students have all the months of their calendars completed, they fasten their calendar pages together and make an interesting cover page.

Dealing with Diversities

Cultural and Religious: Here is a great opportunity to capitalize on what these students can bring in the way of symbolization and illustration ideas; they can also talk about what certain special days mean to them. A good idea is to ask them ahead of time so they can practise. Have them talk to the class about a special day related to their religion or culture when it comes time to mark that date on the calendars. This is one of the most authentic and natural ways I have found to celebrate these diversities.

Linguistic: The same suggestions as above may hold true for ESL students. As an example, a child from China with limited English may have wonderful stories to tell about Chinese New Year. Encourage that child to tell the story in the first language rather than stumbling through it in English. The rest of the class will not understand, but it exposes them to another language (always a great idea) and celebrates the student's language. If students know limited English, you may wish to ask them ahead of time to practise one or two sentences in English to share about the events. Either way, celebration of a student's language and culture is the key.

Motivational: These students may enjoy collating the information on their own or with you for additional one-on-one time. Offer this activity to them, being sure to suggest how its completion will be of benefit to you.

Physical: Because of the small areas in which the students are working, any students with hand-eye coordination or manual dexterity problems may need a buddy to help them.

Gifted: Challenge these children to research holidays in more depth. Invite them to write reports on specific holidays that interest them or share findings with the class in any way they want to. They could also find or research appropriate symbols for different holidays (e.g., menorah candles for Hanukkah) to help students when it comes to illustrating specific dates.

Dealing with Developmental Levels

Kindergarten to Grade 3: As mentioned previously, it may be necessary to adapt the size of the working calendar pages. Another idea would be to enlarge just the squares on which you want students to write (see Figure 22). Using fine-pointed coloring tools helps younger students keep their work smaller. Keep in mind, too, the importance of having the information collated before students begin calendar work.

Grades 4 to 9: Invite students to be as creative as possible when decorating their calendars. Let them add important personal dates such as family birthdays, as well.

Making Curriculum Connections and More

Language Arts: Extension activities include researching and writing about any unfamiliar special days, interviewing community members about special days, creating posters about the calendars (especially if the class has a For Sale copy), and writing personal reflections titled "What I Learned" based on compiling the calendars.

Health: Students could take the opportunity to discuss similarities and differences between peoples of different races, cultures, and religions, and to celebrate diversity.

Social Studies: Ways to follow up include locating the parts of the world associated with specific religions or cultures, and learning about traditions and how they affect the dominant culture.

Date _____

Dear Parent/Guardian,

Our class is going to make cultural calendars, and we need your help. These calendars will provide valuable information for all of us about the many wonderful diversities in our classroom. The calendars will also show many of this year's important school activities, as well as every child's birthday.

Please help your child complete the "Special Days Family Survey" as soon as possible and ensure the survey's return to class. You may also use the back of the page.

If there are any special days you feel comfortable talking to the class about, please let me know by filling in the related section below. Thank you for your cooperation and assistance.

Sincerely,

I would be interested in talking to the class about _____

I am available _____

You may contact me at _____

Name of Parent/Guardian _____

Special Days Family Survey

Special Day	Date	Religious/ Traditional Basis	Purpose/ Description	Foods	Related Symbols

Tell Me a Story

Friends, Romans, countrymen, lend me your ears …

What This Project Addresses

- speaking and listening
- story grammar, story structure, and story mapping
- appreciation of others
- self-confidence and self-concept
- cultural diversity
- curriculum connections: Language Arts, Social Studies, Drama

Project Overview

"Tell me a story." What familiar words these are! Many of us have pleasant memories of sitting on a grandmother's knee listening to wonderful, often whimsical stories that we wished would never end. (Indeed, some of them never *did* seem to end.)

Our students are just like we were, in this respect at least. They love being told stories and I think teachers, their plates already overflowing with curriculum and extracurricular demands, tend to overlook this excellent teaching/learning strategy. Some children, like some adults, are natural storytellers; others—not so much. But natural storyteller or not, everyone will gain from this project which teaches and encourages storytelling in the classroom.

It is interesting to note that Latino and First Nations children tend to be much better storytellers than children from western cultures. This may be due to the increased emphasis we put on reading, as opposed to storytelling; by so doing perhaps we have contributed to the squelching of young imaginations—a much debated educational topic. These same Latino and First Nations children, however, come from cultures where children were taught through stories, and most of these stories did not have the traditional beginning, middle, and ending that Europeans have come to expect. This poses an interesting situation when it comes to storytelling in class, where we begin by analysing simple stories through story mapping and grammar. By doing this, we give children a tool for creating their own stories to tell. This is the perfect time to point out the wonderful cultural diversity within a classroom and explain these differences in what we have come to see as basic story structure.

Here is a quick review of the aforementioned terms that are taught to students to give them a "sense of story" and to provide them with a predictable story structure:

- *Story grammar* is an outline that summarizes the main story events, characters, settings, plot and climax, as well as the beginning, middle, and end. (Point out that Aboriginals do not have a clearly defined ending or resolution to their stories.)
- *Story mapping* is a visual depiction of the story action, setting, characters, and so on. The process emphasizes individual interpretations and helps point out that there are many ways to develop stories: different students "visualize" the same story differently and their illustrations reflect that.

Although professional storytellers may argue that storytellers only subtly suggest and do not need "effects" to hold people's attention, many students need the extra support that comes from use of gestures and sound effects. It may be a good idea to discuss both storytelling styles with the students.

Remember, too, that for a storytelling to be effective, it must have these elements:

- a simple plot
- a clear problem or conflict
- repetition of ideas, words, or phrases
- enough action to generate lots of gestures
- sound effects—music background or vocal sounds such as a dog barking
- characters easily defined

TINY TRUE TALE

The tired teacher was just leaving her classroom when she saw a young man sitting on the floor in the hall. It was late and he should have been home ages ago. "Rory," she exclaimed. "Why are you still here?" Rory was a First Nations boy who struggled with reading and writing, but was always quiet and cooperative in class.

"Waitin' for you, teacher," Rory said as he stood up, his height, tall for his age, almost dwarfing the tiny Grade 6 teacher. "Wanted to tell you somethin'."

"Why didn't you just come into the room and tell me?"

"You were workin', teacher. I didn't want to disturb you."

"Oh Rory, well, never mind, tell me now."

"Wanted to tell you thanks for letting me tell my stories today. No teacher ever let me do that before. I got lots of stories. My grandfather told them to me. So—thanks. That's all."

The teacher, momentarily dumbstruck, mumbled, "You're welcome, Rory," and watched the boy walk toward the door. Today had been story-telling day and Rory, much to everyone's delight, had told several very interesting stories about the spirits of the earth, the Medicine Circle, and the animals. She hadn't even realized just how important that experience had been to Rory. She vowed to have more such days in the future.

Materials

- a couple of stories to "tell" (See the brief example below.)

Lost in the Woods

One day a man was hiking in the woods when he suddenly realized he was lost. After trying for hours to find his way home, he finally sat down on a rock in a clearing and put his head in his hands, ready to stay there until he died.

Soon another man entered the clearing. "What's wrong," he asked. "Are you lost?"

"Yes," answered the first man. "Are you lost too?"

"Yes," replied the second man, but he didn't look upset. Instead, he was smiling.

"If you're lost, then why are you smiling?" the first man asked.

"Because," replied the second man, "now there are two of us and if you will take my hand, together we will find the way home."

And they did!

When encouraging students to practise storytelling, just be sensitive to any students who never feel ready to share a story aloud. You may need to plan an alternative activity for them, such as reciting a poem or reading aloud a short selection.

Steps for Teachers

1. Introduce the project by telling a story such as the short one above or by inviting an elder or storyteller from the community to come to class to tell a story. After the telling, lead a discussion about storytelling and its many merits, such as the following:

   - reinforcement of listening and speaking skills
   - encouragement of creativity and imagination
   - reinforcement of need for enunciation, expression, and enthusiasm when telling
   - reinforcement and practice of story forms
   - personal connections between teller and audience through eye contact

2. Discuss story grammar and story mapping in as much detail as your class can handle. With younger children it may be enough to talk about beginning, middle, and end. With older students, a more detailed examination of terms and events is important. (See the definitions of story grammar and story mapping above.)
3. Divide students into pairs. Allow free talk time about stories they might be able to tell. *Give them a few days to find and practise a story to tell their partners.*
4. Allow students to work first with their partners, then in small groups; then, if they are willing, let them tell their stories to the whole class. Make this a real celebration of their efforts.

Quick Check: Tell Me a Story

- Have I checked to see whether any students need help choosing a story?
- Am I well attuned to the comfort levels of my students as storyteller performers?

Steps for Students

1. Students think of good stories they would like to tell and discuss them with their partners. They may make notes or write the stories out if they want to.
2. Students first practise telling their stories to their partners. They should give each other pointers on things like speaking clearly, loudly, and with expression, and ideas on things like sound effects if they choose to use them.
3. Students then tell their stories to a small group of classmates.
4. If desired, they may also tell their stories to the whole class.

Dealing with Diversities

Cultural: Strongly encourage them to tell stories about or from their own cultures and then take time to discuss and celebrate these stories with the whole class.

Linguistic: Allow ESL students to tell stories in their first languages. Even if they know some English, the stories will be more animated, more flowing, and generally more enjoyable to share and listen to if these students tell them in the languages they are most comfortable with.

Intellectual: These students may be better off remembering a very short story and practising with you first. Remembering is often difficult for them, but having to think about the story facts quickly may be even more difficult. In *Speaking Rules!*, Cathy Miyata reports that these students have more luck with storytelling than public speaking because stories are meant to be told and tend to have lots of patterning. Avoid putting the students in any situation that seems uncomfortable; if necessary, find an alternative type of presentation.

Motivational and Behavioral: If these students balk at this project (and it is one of the very few they may react negatively to), suggest that they share something else, such as a favorite piece of music, screened by you first, and then talk a little about it.

Dealing with Developmental Levels

Kindergarten to Grade 3: These children are natural storytellers, but if they are having problems, help them narrow the topic, for example, telling a story about a pet, or suggest a retelling of a familiar story, such as a folk or fairy tale.

Grades 4 to 9: Encourage them to research and find good stories for retelling. If some students truly prefer to tell their own, point out that it will take much more time for them to write and revise the stories thoroughly first and that traditional stories provide good models.

Making Curriculum Connections and More

Language Arts: Students could write out from memory the story that someone else told. They could make comparison charts between stories that are told and stories that are written or compare traditional structured stories to stories from cultures that don't follow the clear beginning, middle, and end pattern. Students could also compile what they learned about story grammar while preparing to tell stories.

Social Studies: This project provides an opportunity to discuss how other people pass on their culture and history through stories. Students could research storytelling from different civilizations, countries, and cultures.

Drama: Students may explore ways of making their storytelling more interesting to others. They could consider adding music and gestures, for example, and once satisfied, share their stories with neighboring classes, especially younger ones.

4 Projects That Emphasize Synthesis

With the exception of Evaluation, Synthesis, according to Bloom, is the highest level of thinking. It is the putting together of known, understood, and analysed material and concepts to create new wholes.

Since the products that demonstrate Synthesis are many and varied, student success in this area is difficult to determine objectively. Any student work that is unique and individual can be considered in terms of Synthesis. Questions beginning with *why* provide clues to Synthesis, as do questions with leads such as these: *What makes you think that …,* or *How does this work …*

Many of the projects described in earlier chapters involve elements of Synthesis. However, the projects selected for this chapter depend more on student synthesis of data and material in order to create the unique finished pieces than do the others. These projects truly involve "the whole child."

The following represents the main skill clusters in the projects in this chapter:

Silent Island Building: Students will need to take risks as no oral communication is allowed. They will have to adapt habits and communicate in an unfamiliar manner. They will imagine, adapt, plan, and create a mysterious, clay island.

Small Personal Inuksuit: Students will design and rearrange stones in order to emulate authentic Inuit inuksuit and to communicate messages in much the same way as the stone figures in the North do.

Balloon Balls: Students will integrate and modify what they know about the characteristics of balloons in order to create original and imaginative balls.

Photo Story-books: Students will plan, combine, and integrate photographs and text in order to compose an original book that communicates a message.

Heritage Home Display: Students will plan, create, design and integrate information with materials to construct model houses. They will negotiate and collaborate with peers in the process.

My Maleta, My Box of Memories: Students will combine, integrate, rearrange, and adapt a variety of materials to form a compilation of artifacts representative of themselves and their school year. They will speculate and anticipate as they choose resources.

Lid-scape Landscapes: Students will collaborate, negotiate, generalize and construct in order to create landscapes in miniature with their peers.

Fantasy Sandcastles: Students will communicate and facilitate while modifying and adapting materials in an imaginative pursuit of the perfect sandcastle.

Spectacular School Brochures: Students will collaborate, integrate, plan, propose, prepare, and emulate while creating school flyers. They will also anticipate the needs and interests of others to whom the flyers will be given.

Silent Island Building

Give thy thoughts no tongue.

What This Project Addresses

- careful observation
- cooperation and problem solving
- team and group work; appreciation of the benefits gained from shared effort and cooperation
- empathy for feelings of isolation
- non-verbal communication
- patience and perseverance
- curiosity, creativity, and inventiveness
- curriculum connections: Language Arts, Health, Social Studies, Science

Project Overview

Have you ever noticed how children enjoy games that involve being blindfolded? It forces them to focus on their other senses, and, at the same time, creates a sense of mystery and excitement. If we temporarily remove one of the other senses—auditory, for instance—the same positive reactions occur. Children also gain a sense of what it might be like to lose or lack that particular sense or ability.

Often children, unless they are newcomers themselves, have little or no understanding of what it is like for a new or in any way "different" student in the classroom. This project forces them to experience some of the frustration of not being able to *communicate* with peers about a project they must do together. In other words, in small groups they are to *create* something, in this case a fantasy island, *in complete silence.* They will need to mime or somehow make their intentions known to one another by whatever means they can. No writing is allowed either!

In brief, students are given the basic direction "build any kind of island you want to," placed in groups, and provided with various supplies. The results are amazing.

Once the islands are built, debriefing opens up all kinds of thoughts and ideas about frustrations experienced, how they were handled, how these ideas may apply to others, and so on. Students also talk readily about how they solved (or didn't solve) conflicts or problems, and how excited they felt when something came together properly. "Silent Island Building" is an eye-opening experience.

TINY TRUE TALE

After the project was completed and students were allowed to reflect freely:
John: *Wow, was that ever hard! I thought you guys were making a volcano, but then I saw the boat and I realized it must be a different kind of island.*
Heather: *I knew you didn't understand. Boys never understand.*
John: *How come you got to be the leader anyway, Heather?*
Heather: *No one else got started.*
Jill: *That's how all leaders get to be. No one else gets started.*
Heather: *Yeah.*
John: *Maybe. But next time, figure out a better way to make me understand. I was really confused and that made me feel mad.*

Ask the students what it would be like if they couldn't talk or write notes to communicate. Point out that this is how non-English-speaking newcomers to the country must feel. From there, introduce the island building project.

Materials

- enough play dough or modelling clay to supply about two handfuls per group
- cardboard squares, about 30 cm wide, one per group
- pieces of stick, bark, rocks, gravel, and sand put into baggies, one per group
- information and pictures of typical islands, such as Vancouver Island, a volcanic island, a "single palm tree" island with shipwrecked person, and a rocky island covered with seals
- white glue
- scissors
- scraps of green and brown felt, as can be purchased at dollar stores

Steps for Teachers

1. Gather necessary materials for the projects. You might ask students to collect materials such as rocks and bark, as well. Make one cardboard square, approximately 30 cm to 40 cm on each side, per group, as well.
2. Predetermine the members of each group. It is a good idea to keep the groups as heterogeneous as possible, with a student who is a "natural leader" in each one. The hope is that this person will help the group move past the initial how-do-we-communicate problem more quickly.
3. Explain to students that they will be taking part in an exercise to help them to understand what it is like to come from a different country and not understand the culture or language. All communication within the groups must be non-verbal.
4. Share pictures of various islands and discuss. Remind the students that once they are given the signal to start, they cannot say a single word or write any notes.

Quick Check: Silent Island Building

- Is my play dough or modelling clay stiff enough to hold its shape? (I have had disasters with too soft dough that *morphs* down from a mountain to a mud pool.)
- Are garbage bags available for cleanup?
- Have I prepared the groups and decided where each group will work?

Steps for Students

1. Their task is to build a fantasy island—any kind of island—in their groups, using only their eyes. They may use all their materials or just some of them. All group members must be involved. The time limit is 20 minutes.
2. If they see something, such as a particular piece of wood, that another group has, and would like it, they have to find a way to get it without talking or stealing.
3. Each group chooses one person to speak for it at the end of the building session.

Dealing with Diversities

Linguistic: ESL students make the best leaders for this project, as all others are "on their playing field" and no one can speak.

Physical: Depending on their personal challenges, these students can usually become fully involved in this activity.

Behavioral: If a few students tend to be "overactive," put them in charge of groups. By giving them the responsibility of ensuring that their groups' islands are well done, you will often reduce inappropriate behavior.

Gifted: Invite these students to compile the information gleaned through debriefing discussions into a chart that can be posted in the room. The chart might be titled "Ways to Communicate Without Words."

Dealing with Developmental Levels

Kindergarten to Grade 3: Keep the groups to no more than four students each. Some children may be best working at this project with a partner, not a group; they would then have only one other person with whom to communicate non-verbally.

Grades 4 to 9: Teachers may be afraid to use this type of "play dough" activity with older students, but students of all ages thoroughly enjoy the experience. These children can handle larger groups.

Making Curriculum Connections and More

Language Arts: The project opens up many opportunities for writing, such as

- writing lists of ways for "helping newcomers"
- writing poetry describing the fantasy islands
- writing stories about the islands (or illustrating them)
- writing reports on the steps involved in the building of an island
- creating an advertisement about a fantasy island

Health: This project leads into writing personal reflections on problem solving, discussing why it's hard to make needs met at times, and listing or recording in some way suggestions for improving non-verbal communication.

Social Studies: Students could learn about cultural differences and how people feel and act when they immigrate. They could carry out surveys of the nationalities, ethnic backgrounds, and first languages represented in the class, school, or community, and discuss the importance of having an awareness of living in a multicultural, multi-linguistic society. They might also make "group function" charts reviewing how well members worked together.

Science: From making fantasy islands, the class could go on to learn about real islands, volcanoes, and rock formations.

Silent Writing: An alternative project is to use the same Eyes-Only technique and have groups create posters, signs, or illustrations of something recently studied, or of a story read. It is even possible, with older students, to have them write a poem as a group, without speaking at all. They love it and all are involved.

Small Personal Inuksuit

Blow, blow, thou winter wind …

What This Project Addresses

- cultural symbols (specifically Inuit culture)
- cultural awareness, respect, and appreciation
- problem solving and perseverance
- creativity, self-concept, and personal identity
- curriculum connections: Language Arts, Social Studies, Science, Mathematics

Project Overview

Have you ever given thought to just how many means of communication we have today? Only a few years ago, being able to *see* the person you were calling on a miniature cell phone was science fiction. With technology moving with lightning speed, it is sometimes a good idea to step back and enjoy something more connected to the earth. "Small Personal Inuksuit" is such a project.

Inuksuit (plural; *Ee-nook-sweet*) are sacred symbols of Inuit culture as well as being forms of communication. The word "inuksuk" (singular) means like a man or to act in the capacity of a man. It comes from the Inuit word "inuk" meaning human being. (See Figure 23.)

Typically, these rock arrangements are found in the North as guides to travellers, but they can be used for a variety of purposes. Here are some other possible uses of inuksuit:

- as astronomy signs pointing to the North Star
- as indicators of caribou crossing
- as indicators of places where spirits (good or evil) reside
- as markings for a place of celebration or festival
- as markings or warnings of possible danger, such as falling rocks or thin ice
- as message boards and ways of welcoming others
- as burial markers and as memorials
- as pointers to something of importance or significance
- if placed closely together, as a way to represent a "circle of friends" or family
- if set in a semi-circle, as a way to herd caribou

The meaning is up to the builder: inuksuit can be playful, spiritual, or serious. It should be noted that the Nunavut territorial flag is decorated with the symbol of an inuksuk.

Inuksuit, made of carefully selected stones, are held together by the balance and weight of the stones themselves. For classroom purposes, it is better to join the stones with a fixative, but it should be pointed out that the Inuit do not rely on "glue." In the classroom, calking putty holds the stones well. It lasts for a few days, but may not endure much handling and eventually the statues fall. By first putting white glue between the touching stone, then using the putty *around* the glue (see Figure 24), you will have a permanent fixative.

An Inuksuk

Figure 23

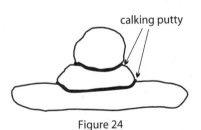

calking putty

Figure 24

Every student in the class had made an inuksuk, and all were different. For the evening of Open House, two students took it upon themselves to create an appropriate environment for the inuksuit and spent all day arranging cotton batten on a card table to look like snow. They studiously placed several of the more "human" looking inuksuit in a circle to represent the friendships in the class. They made signs and even igloos from sugar cubes, without any encouragement from me. That evening they proudly showed off their Inuit environment. The amazing thing was that both students were what I would have considered "motivationally diverse" or, at times, "behaviorally diverse." Most of the time, neither student was keen to do much of anything in class. It was thrilling to watch them become captivated with the little inuksuit.

Materials

A good resource for this project is the beautiful picture book *Make Your Own Inuksuk* by Mary Wallace (Toronto: Maple Tree Press).

- a variety of small rocks collected by students (7 to 10 rocks per student)
- strips of calking putty, not the soft packaged kind
- white glue (optional)
- picture or overhead of an inuksuk (see Figure 23)
- pail, old towel, and water for washing rocks

Steps for Teachers

Open a discussion about ways we let others know what we're doing. Students will likely mention leaving messages on answering machines or on the fridge, or text messaging. Lead from this to the way that the Inuit have been leaving messages in the North for countless years. Then invite the students to "think like the Inuit" and build a personal messenger.

1. Make an inuksuk as a sample and motivational tool, or locate a good picture of an inuksuk—there are many on the Internet.
2. Cut out pieces of cardboard, about 10 cm to 15 cm square, one per student. Also, divide calking putty into individual portions and wrap tightly in plastic wrap.
3. Introduce the project, being sure to point out the difference between the relative permanence of an inuksuk as opposed to a text message, for example. Learning what an inuksuk is can be a class activity, where you provide the information, or an individual research project, depending on age, interest, and time.

Quick Check: Small Personal Inuksuit

- Is the calking putty fresh? (soft, as opposed to old and dried out)
- Do I have water, an old towel, and a bowl to wash any rock that may have sand or dirt adhered to it?
- Do I have a supply of "extra" rocks for students who might need a different shape or size?

Steps for Students

An excellent culminating activity for this project is to make and strategically place a "class inuksuk," using large rocks.

1. Students collect 7 to 10 rocks that they really like, including two that are flat.
2. They then learn more about inuksuit, either from the teacher or on their own. They choose a specific "purpose" for their inuksuit *before* building them.
3. Students wash their rocks and dry them carefully. They choose a flat rock that is slightly bigger than the others as the base, or bottom, and arrange the rocks to suit their purpose. As they work, they may use small pieces of soft putty to stick rocks together.

Dealing with Diversities

Cultural: This is an excellent project for incorporation of symbolism of other cultures; invite these students to share culturally specific symbolic art forms, or similar communication devices or ideas. Draw on the knowledge of elders or parents who may be able to supply additional information about the child's culture.

Linguistic: Use a model (yours) as well as pictures. Be sure to explain the project verbally and visually. Encourage ESL students to work with an English-speaking peer, and, if necessary, with an interpreter.

Motivational: Invite these students to be in charge of the final display of inuksuit (see **Tiny True Tale** on page 109). Generally the intrinsic motivation of this project is enough, but you might give these students the responsibility of distributing the putty or of helping any less capable students, perhaps students with physical diversities.

Physical: Provide a buddy, either an older student or a volunteer, to help with this task.

Behavioral: Take caution to avoid the possible "throwing" of rocks, by first agreeing on class rules for this project. (Avoid saying "no throwing" as that may plant the seed; instead, focus on positive rules.) Since it is a hands-on task, usually all students want to be involved. Perhaps more active children could be put in charge of the "rock washing" or could help peers who may be having difficulty.

Gifted: Invite them to try creating their inuksuit without bonding material (using weight and balance only), or to research further the use of inuksuit in the Inuit culture.

Dealing with Developmental Levels

Kindergarten to Grade 3: Use smaller stones that are easy to manage, and soft calking putty. Be sure at least some of the stones have a flat surface to simplify the adhering.

Grades 4 to 9: Independent research *before* students embark on the task is often helpful.

Making Curriculum Connections and More

Language Arts: Among the many writing extensions are these:

- dialogue journalling between peers about their inuksuit
- writing personal reflections after the creation of the inuksuit
- writing stories about the life of the inuksuk in the North (For example: Does a storm or a caribou stampede break or damage an inuksuk? Does a "navigation" inuksuk point the way and save a weary traveller from falling through thin ice?)
- writing from the point of view of an inuksuk (*What does it see/witness?*)
- writing conversations (correct use of conventions such as quotation marks) between inanimate objects, two inuksuit who have seen many things

Students could also explore the formation of uncommon plurals, such as going from *inuksuk* to *inuksuit*.

Social Studies: Creating an inuksuk is a good way to lead into learning about Inuit culture or comparing methods of communication between peoples in different cultures around the world. The class could also brainstorm methods of communication used in today's world and then make comparisons between methods. For example, inuksuit are durable compared to greeting cards, e-mail, and faxed messages. Students could explore how human needs, such as the need to communicate, are met in various cultures.

Science: "Small Personal Inuksuit" leads naturally into studying rock forms, types, and formations, as well as examining the effects of heat and cold on land, ice, and rocks. Students could also study weather patterns in the North and record lists of words specific to northern climates.

Mathematics: The students could take the opportunity to study matters of weight, pressure, and balance.

Balloon Balls

As merry as the day is long ... these little balls bring smiles.

What This Project Addresses

- coordination and hand-eye dexterity
- direction following
- creativity
- respect for living things and the environment
- curriculum connections: Language Arts, Health, Science, Physical Education

Project Overview

We are all likely aware of the wonderful Chinese chime balls that you roll around in the hand to relieve stress and create inner "balance." This project stems from them, even though in this case the finished products are anything but hard steel. They are small, soft, squishy balls that fit nicely in the palm of the hand, any hand.

Using small baggies, a handful of rice, and a couple of balloons, each student can make a little, squishy ball (not unlike the soft stress balls sold in stores). All it takes is about ten minutes and then the fun and the learning begin.

Each finished ball is the color of the last balloon used, with little circles cut in it to reveal the color(s) of the underlying balloons. Some students get really creative and add more decorations to the balls with felt pens, but this is not necessary. The nice thing is that the balls can be given as gifts to parents, friend, guardians, and even the school principal or secretary, making this an authentic, purposeful project.

TINY TRUE TALE

The Grade 3 class had completed their balloon balls and were busily writing notes to the people who were to receive their little gifts. It was close to Christmas, so the class had decided to give the balloon balls away as Christmas gifts. One young man was not writing, but instead was busy squeezing his ball over and over with his hands, elbows, behind his knees, even between his shoulder and ear. When asked why he was not writing, his response was, "I decided to keep this little ball for me. It's doing a good job of getting rid of my stress so I figure that's about as good a gift as any for my mom."

Show Chinese steel balls or soft stress balls, if you have them. Otherwise, discuss what sorts of things people do to relieve stress (make themselves feel better). Gradually, lead the discussion toward the concept of the little soft balls, and tell the students that each of them is going to make one. Allow students to pick two or three colored balloons and then watch the excitement.

Materials

- a bag of rice—between 1400 g and 2000 g is plenty for a class
- baggies with fold-over tops—*not* the zip-lock kind
- enough balloons to give every student about three
- scissors

Steps for Teachers

1. Make a ball yourself so you know exactly how it works—it is amazingly easy. Follow the student steps on the next page. (See Figure 25.)

2. Put the rice into a large container so students can stick their hands into it. The rule is "one handful per balloon ball." In this way, the finished product exactly fits little hands. Or, if you are working with Grade 1 or 2 students, it may be wise to prepare the baggies ahead of time as sometimes the students can't tie them.

3. When students are working, circulate to check for "cutting through to the rice," which will mean having to start over. Encouraging them to help each other by "pinching out a little piece of balloon for your neighbor to cut" helps to avoid this.

Quick Check: Balloon Balls

- Do I have enough balloons to allow for some tearing and breaking?
- Are the scissors sharp enough to snip the balloons?
- Have I decided on a purpose for this task? (What will we do with the balloon balls?)

Steps for Students

1. Students each put a handful of rice into a baggie and tie the top. It is important not to tie the baggie too tightly. A little space is needed between rice and knot. Students roll the baggies in their hands to make balls.

2. Students cut the necks off two or three balloons of different colors and then stretch one balloon over the baggie. The open neck forms a circle showing the baggie through it. They then stretch a second balloon over the first, being sure to cover the "baggie circle." Now the color of the first balloon shows through.

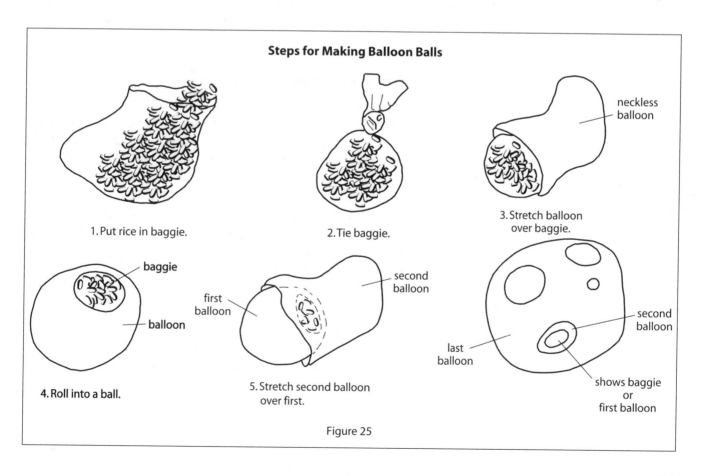

Steps for Making Balloon Balls

1. Put rice in baggie.

2. Tie baggie.

3. Stretch balloon over baggie.

neckless balloon

4. Roll into a ball.

baggie

balloon

5. Stretch second balloon over first.

first balloon

second balloon

last balloon

second balloon

shows baggie
or
first balloon

Figure 25

3. Students can either add one more balloon, or begin cutting very small holes in the outside balloon. They do this by pinching up a tiny piece of the outside balloon and snipping it off. They may have to work with a partner. Each time they snip, a little circle of a different color peeks through. If students cut through to the rice, they'll have to start again.

Dealing with Diversities

Linguistic: Allow these students to be close to you when you demonstrate the steps. They will be able to follow without understanding all the language.

Physical: Arrange for an aide to be present to assist these children, if necessary.

Motivational and Behavioral: If these children are allowed to cut the necks off all the balloons ahead of time, it often creates a desire to complete their own projects with little prompting.

Gifted: Invite these students to research Chinese steel balls and share their findings with the class (unless there are Chinese students in the room, in which case you could ask them to share this information).

Dealing with Developmental Levels

Kindergarten to Grade 3: As mentioned earlier, it may be necessary for an adult to fill baggies and tie ahead of time. It is also a good idea to have younger students work with a partner when it comes to pulling up the balloon to snip small holes.

Grades 4 to 9: Encourage creativity by suggesting they try cutting a variety of shapes or using several balloons and cutting in the same place more than once to get a "color rings" effect.

Making Curriculum Connections and More

Language Arts and Health: After doing this project, students could do research about the effects of stress and ways to relieve it (squeezing the balls is one way). They could also do various kinds of writing: the sequence of steps in balloon-ball creation, including the cautions about accidentally snipping the baggie; comparisons of various classmates' balloon balls; and letters explaining the uses of balloon balls, to accompany balloon balls when they are given away.

Science: Extensions include discussing or researching the possible disastrous effects on birds or small animals if they eat the uncooked rice and why it is necessary to keep the balloon balls away from pets; experimenting with the flexibility or stretch-ability of various balloons (some colors have more flexibility than others); and discussing or researching food chains, and how human actions can threaten the survival of other living things.

Physical Education: Students could learn to juggle with the balloon balls, toss several balls back and forth at the same time to improve manual dexterity and coordination, or toss the balloon balls at targets.

Photo-Storybooks

This above all—to thine own self be true.

What This Project Addresses

- individuality and personal values
- creativity
- storytelling; communicating ideas through a variety of ways
- book knowledge
- personal pride
- curriculum connections: Language Arts, Health, possibly Social Studies and Science depending on book "themes"

"Photo-Storybooks" lends itself to any and all curriculum areas. Simply delineate the "umbrella theme" for the content of the story. For instance, if studying electricity in Science, tell students that the photo-storybook must relate to electricity.

Project Overview

There's not a child anywhere who wouldn't like to be the hero in a book. Now every student in your class can be just that!

Creating individual (or partner) photo-stories has been the highlight of many students' early school years, as the resulting books are lasting reminders of that time. We all know just how much children love to see themselves in photos and to hear their names in stories. You might recall the popular children's books based on writing a child's name into the story and making the child the protagonist—how much children love such books. The "Photo-Storybook" project capitalizes on this idea as photos of the students are written about and made into books.

There are two possible approaches, depending on the ages of the students. You can take a number of candid photos of students in various poses, or the children themselves can be given cameras to take the photos. Then the photos are arranged in some sort of sequence, glued to paper, one per page, and appropriate comments or a "story" is added.

I strongly suggest that you do the project yourself first. Take a few random photos (or borrow a few from albums) and write a story to fit them. Put the text and pictures together and voilà—a photo-storybook! If you have time, you may follow the pattern used with older students and write your story first. Just keep in mind the time required to process photos if you choose this pattern.

Older students should write their stories first, then set out to take appropriate pictures. If two or three work together, they can be camera-people for one another. Younger children can be given three or four photos of themselves and helped to write little stories based on them.

There are a number of ways to create the books.

- Use loose pages for photo albums with the clear paper that adheres to itself. Slide both the photo and the paper with the appropriate text on each page.
- Use technology and digital cameras (many schools now have these available for teacher/student use) and do all the work with computers.
- Photocopy the photos with a color copier so that they can easily be glued to an ordinary page; pages can then be tied together or coiled.

Although this project may seem like a lot of work, it really isn't and the results are well worth any minor issues, such as who gets to use the camera next, that may occur. The finished books, for which students create titles, covers, an author biography page, even a pretend publication page, are treasures that make wonderful gifts for parents, guardians, community seniors, or the students themselves. This is a never-fail project!

TINY TRUE TALE

There's always a student the teacher feels she or he hasn't reached— the one who comes to school regularly, but never seems to learn anything, or even be interested in anything. Louis was one of those. He never caused any trouble; he just existed in my class. When we made photo-storybooks, he cooperated (he always cooperated) and when his book was complete and other students were excitedly discussing what they were going to do with their wonderful books, Louis just quietly put his in his backpack. One student asked him what he had planned for his book. He shrugged and looked uninterested.

Several years later I got a surprise e-mail from Louis. I may not have remembered him had he not taken time to describe himself as "the boy who never did much in your Grade 6 class at …" He went on to say how much pleasure both he and his grandparents (with whom he lived) still got from his photo-storybook, and to thank me profusely for allowing him to take part in that project. Of course, I cried my eyes out. Who wouldn't?

Materials

Ask students if any of them have ever had a book written about them. If some have had "put-in-your-own-name" books, invite them to share their feelings about these. Then lead the discussion toward being the heroes of their own books, and show all or part of your own photo-storybook.

- cameras (even the disposable ones which are not too costly if several students share)
- paper for book pages, such as colored paper, card, or photo album pages
- method of fastening pages together, such as coils and coiler, ribbon, string, or staples
- glue sticks for attaching pictures
- a color photocopying machine, if possible
- heavier card for covers
- coloring mediums, such as markers, bright crayons, and oil pastels, for covers
- access to computers and laminators, if desired

Steps for Teachers

1. Make a sample book (or at least a few pages) of your own. I found that making overhead transparencies of a couple of pages allowed the whole class to see what I was talking about and gave everyone a good start.
2. Arrange access to cameras for all students. Check first to see how many already have access.
3. Decide on a story theme if you so choose. This works well with older students; with younger students, it's better to allow them to come up with ideas based on photos. Possible themes include friendship, sharing, having fun, and helping others. Or, if you want to connect to a Science or Social Studies topic, such themes as avoiding pollution, community awareness, and ecosystems can guide the students and give them ideas about where to focus their picture taking.

4. Find a good picture book, like *The Rough-faced Girl* by Rafe Martin, read it to the class, and point out to students how the pictures help the story content. This will set the stage for students preparing their own photo-stories.
5. As a class, discuss ways the pages can be put together to form a real book.

Quick Check: Photo-Storybooks

- Do I have enough cameras, or know which children will not have access to cameras on their own?
- Do the students clearly know what I expect of them? (In other words, for this complicated project, are my directions clear?)

Steps for Students

1. Students may write their stories first or take pictures and then write their stories.
2. Students decide on a sequence for their pictures. They need to make the story they want to tell and their pictures fit together. They can dress up and "act out" events in the story if they want to.
3. For the text part of their books, they use their best printing or writing, or do word processing. They also make author biography pages for the end of their books, think of good titles, and design covers.
4. Students fasten their books together and prepare to share them with classmates.

Dealing with Diversities

Cultural: Encourage these students to write books about their own cultures. In this way when you share and celebrate the books, you will be celebrating cultural diversity as well.

Linguistic: Allow these children to write the text in their first languages or in a combination of first and second languages. This celebrates the first languages and creates a learning situation for everyone in the class.

Religious: If these students are comfortable with it, encourage them to include aspects of their religious beliefs. For example, a Muslim student took a picture of her parents in traditional dress and then described the religious activity in which they were partaking. This kind of sharing creates a great learning situation for all.

Socio-economic: If you are expecting students to come up with their own photos, be sure that these children have access to cameras and developing money. Perhaps there is a school budget to help with this. If not, consider approaching a local supermarket for "gifts" of disposable cameras—even if past their "best before" dates, they still work well. You might also solicit help from local groups. The amount of money required is not extreme and usually people are willing to help.

Intellectual: Help these children to organize the stories they want to tell. Provide scribes if necessary as the final copies must be something that makes them feel proud.

Physical: Be sensitive when suggesting personal photographs. Some of these children do not like their pictures taken; others don't mind at all. Check this out individually with the student(s) early in the project. If they prefer no photos, find an alternative such as taking photos of a pet and writing the story about it.

Gifted: Although these students usually love this activity and write amazing, complicated stories, a few have wanted to write expository text instead. Accept this willingly.

Dealing with Developmental Levels

Kindergarten to Grade 3: As a rule, very young students are better working from the photos and writing as much as they can about each photo. Teachers can take the photos, being sure to get several of each child alone and encouraging a bit of "acting" during the picture-taking. In this way the children will have a variety of poses to write about.

Grades 4 to 9: Encourage these students to write the stories first and then take appropriate photos. They are masters at this and once they get going, motivation will not be an issue.

Making Curriculum Connections and More

There is so much inherent learning in this project that I will suggest only a few extensions here.

Language Arts: Among the numerous extensions for students are these:

- creating blurbs "selling" the books
- creating a name and synopsis for a possible sequel
- making a list of new spelling words uncovered while writing the book
- writing a business letter to a publisher explaining the book and asking for it to be published
- using story grammar and story mapping to develop beginning, middle, and end, and more
- sharing books in an Authors' Circle, where students sit in a circle, the author reads his or her book, then others ask questions
- listing in sequence the steps to creating a photo-storybook, whether through words or illustrations (for a very young child to follow)
- writing a script based on the book, and choosing real-life movie stars to play the parts (*Who would play the author?*)

Social Studies: Students may come to appreciate and celebrate diverse cultures better by listening to the photo-storybooks of peers.

Heritage Home Display

What This Project Addresses

- heritage, cultural diversity
- common basic needs
- ancestral backgrounds
- research and group cooperation skills
- problem solving
- curriculum connections: Language Arts, Social Studies, Science

Project Overview

Students of all ages like to "build stuff." This project capitalizes on that common interest and invites them to find out about their own heritage, then come together in small groups or with a partner, to construct a likeness of an ancestral house, building, or hut.

The idea is to have students constructing different types of "homes" from the past (or in some cases, today) from all around the world. Once they "discover their roots"—and for some students, the recent immigrants, for instance, this will be easy—they then research to find what might have been a "typical" home in that country a long time ago. The further back in history the students research, the more simplistic the dwelling will be. You may have to help younger children with this search, but from about Grade 3 on, they enjoy doing it themselves. Ask the librarian to pull relevant books ahead of time.

Here is a list of types of dwellings that are relatively simple to construct and that I have seen students in various grades make:

- log cabin
- teepee
- thatched roof cottage
- cave
- tree house
- house on stilts
- igloo
- homestead, farmhouse
- Polynesian-style thatched roof circular hut
- mud house (small, square)
- castle

Once the children have a host of ideas about "old-time-houses," as they often call them, break them into groups, the members of each coming from similar backgrounds, if possible. Assign a different type of home to each group. Some students may elect to be part of a specific group just because they have an interest in the home being constructed there. Use your professional judgment about grouping. Some students may work in pairs, but discourage individual work as the intent is to facilitate authentic communication. Some children may want to help with several different constructions, and will, therefore, want to move from group to group. As long as all are involved, this should be no problem. Keep the groups flexible. See **Dealing with Development Levels** for ideas specific for young children.

Once the constructions are complete, let students arrange them on a tabletop and add appropriate landscaping. You'll be amazed at the finished display. Imaginations really take over and the landscapes around the constructions are often even more creative than the houses themselves.

A Grade 4 girl from Irish descent was informed that her grandparents lived in a brick row house—a row of about thirty houses, all tall, narrow, and identical. Dissatisfied with the idea of building this type of "boring" dwelling, she researched further back in the history of Ireland, and came up with a picture of a lovely thatched-roof cottage, which she and her group proceeded to make.

Another student, a boy born in Canada, but adopted, couldn't find out much about his past, so he ingeniously pointed out that all our ancestors first lived in caves. His group made a great cave out of play dough, which they baked in the oven until it had hardened, then covered with white glue, then sand and rocks. Awesome!

Materials

Involve the students in gathering materials. They will come up with many ideas once they get started.

- popsicle sticks, meat skewers (great for teepees) or any sticks or small pieces of wood
- white glue, hot glue guns, calking putty, thin floral wire, masking tape, thumbtacks, push pins, paper clips, safety pins—anything that will facilitate "fastening" pieces together
- sugar cubes, old Lego pieces or any other children's blocks
- pieces of felt, canvas, burlap or any other fabrics easily obtained
- raffia, dried grasses such as Spanish moss and hay (from craft stores)
- empty toilet tissue or paper towel centres, bubble wrap, small cardboard cartons, and small plastic containers as from yoghurt or deli foodstuffs
- strips of Bristol board or strips cut from cardboard box lids (great for making frames)
- small containers of sand, gravel, pebbles, and river rocks
- clay, Plasticine, or play dough

Steps for Teachers

To introduce the project, ask, "How many of you think your long-ago ancestors lived in caves?" Then, discuss the fact that they probably all did, and go from there.

1. Gathering a variety of materials is the biggest step. Be sure to get a spouse, volunteer, or aide on the case!
2. Try to find a few good picture books that show a variety of different homes. (See Appendix H: Culturally Divergent Books: A Recommended List.) Ask the librarian for help.
3. When you have introduced the project with the "caves" question, discuss with the students the idea that we all have a basic need for shelter and have all come from different ancestors. Lead to a discussion about homes.
4. Once students have gathered information about possible heritage homes, break them into functional, heterogeneous groups, that is, groups that have an equal distribution of students with artistic, creative, and leadership abilities.

Quick Check: Heritage Home Display

- Do the students have a firm grasp of the project?
- Do the students know how they will fasten materials together *before* they start?
- Do I need some extra hands—volunteers, parents, aides, or older students—to help keep things moving smoothly?

Steps for Students

1. Students find out about their pasts—their *distant* pasts. What kind of a home might their ancestors have lived in? They try to find a picture of that type of home.
2. In groups, students decide how they will build the heritage home assigned to them and what supplies they need.
3. One group member draws a sketch of what the finished home will look like. Then the building begins!

Dealing with Diversities

Cultural: This is a great chance for these students to excel and bring interesting facts perhaps unfamiliar to students from the dominant culture.

Linguistic: It is important that ESL students thoroughly understand the requirements of this project so that they won't feel left out once the actual building begins. Find a way to make this happen, perhaps by providing illustrations or by using parents or interpreters.

Physical: If these children are unable to take part in the construction, they can serve as building supervisors.

Gifted: Challenge these students to find the best possible ways to construct the heritage home(s) assigned to their group(s). They can also keep a record of successes and failures during construction, and make this into an interesting story to accompany the finished pieces.

Dealing with Developmental Levels

Kindergarten to Grade 3: If the actual construction of homes is deemed too difficult for these students, find pictures of a variety of heritage homes and have students color them, cut them out, and glue them to small cardboard stands. (A triangle of cardboard glued to the back of a picture will stand it up nicely.) A table-top display can still be made.

An easier alternative for any grade would be to research the homes in the same manner as previously suggested, then make a class book with pictures, illustrations, and even photographs (if there are any heritage homes in the area). It may be possible to photocopy pictures from local archives or newspapers.

Grades 4 to 9: The only caution I would have is to discourage too complicated plans that can lead to frustration. Ask to see the sketches before giving students the OK to build.

Making Curriculum Connections and More

Language Arts: Students may write stories using the facts discovered when researching their individual pasts. They could also write invitations to seniors in the community to visit the class and see the finished display, or record the steps involved in construction.

Social Studies: "Heritage Home Display" leads easily into researching heritages and learning about different lifestyles, cultures, and homes.

Science: Students may explore how different materials bond (or do not bond). They could also come to understand how climate and topography affect habitat.

My Maleta, My Box of Memories

What This Project Addresses

- attention to detail
- location and organization of materials
- appreciation of personal work and achievement
- appreciation of the benefits gained from sharing
- curriculum connections: Language Arts, Health, Social Studies, Art

Project Overview

The idea of creating a personal time capsule is popular. I think we all would like to have a box of memories from our past, a box with an assortment of little things we once treasured. This project allows students to do just that.

A *maleta*, in Spanish, is a suitcase filled with wonderful things. In this instance, it is a small box filled with proof of wonderful student achievements and tiny treasures.

This project is best started early in the year and continued for several months, although of course it can be compressed into a couple of weeks, if desired. Each student brings a small empty box with a lid—namely, a shoebox—decorates it, and fills it with whatever the class decides or the student deems fit to fill it. What goes *in* the maleta can be as varied as the students' imaginations. Suggestions are included below.

Your role will be to find a safe place in the classroom where the many works-in-progress can be stored, and to allow some daily or weekly time for "working on something for the maletas."

The full maleta can first be shared in small groups, then used as a gift for parents, guardians, or community members, or saved as a personal memoir. I have found that most students want to keep the filled boxes for themselves.

TINY TRUE TALE

Kalen worked for three months on his maleta. It was beautifully decorated and filled to capacity with all manner of wonderful things. Some of the more original contents were a feather from the wing of a dead bird he found and buried, a smooth pebble he picked up on a field trip, a rather circuitous summary of a movie watched in class, a piece of broken shoelace with a note explaining he had worn the shoes to win a race on Track and Field Day, and a very grubby Valentine card from a girl called Jenn. Of course, he had a variety of pieces of writing, math sheets, and so on, as well.

Kalen had always said he was filling the maleta for his grandfather who lived in a senior citizens' home, and indeed, the grandfather was the original recipient of the wonderful treasure.

However, (and this part of the tale came from Kalen's mother some years later when her next child was in my class), after a few months, Kalen politely asked his grandfather if he could have the maleta back, assuring the old man that he, Kalen, would keep the maleta safe for him.

Apparently the pull of the wonderful box filled with so many personal memories was more than Kalen could bear!

It is a good idea to put up a poster featuring a list of possible things to put in a maleta. The list should be seen as a reminder only. Also, plan to have a few extra boxes available for those students who might otherwise be empty-handed.

Ask students what a time capsule is and what they'd put in one. Introduce the wonderful word "maleta." If you have a Spanish child in class, invite him or her to share any thoughts and knowledge on the topic.

Materials

- one lidded box per student
- a variety of coloring materials
- glue, scissors, and magazines
- odds and ends such as pieces of ribbon, stickers, and buttons for decorating the boxes
- a story or any material available about time capsules

Steps for Teachers

1. Make a poster identifying possible maleta contents. See the box below.
2. Collect shoeboxes and decorating materials, as not all students will be able to get their own.
3. Discuss the idea of a time capsule and brainstorm ideas about what might go into a personal time capsule.
4. Explain the project to children, pointing out the beautiful Spanish word "maleta." Explain that although the maleta isn't a true time capsule, it is similar in that it will contain memories of the year (or whatever time period is chosen).
5. Have students write an initial item to put into the maleta. A good idea for this first entry is a writing or illustration about the purpose of the maleta. Tell the students that every piece of writing put in the maleta must be as well done as possible, so they should be sure to correct and rewrite, if necessary. In this way, you'll be encouraging them to put only their best work in the boxes.

Things for Your Maleta

- Good pieces of writing
- Special poems
- Good art or pictures you like
- Samples of math worksheets
- Parts (photocopies) of exams or report cards
- Short journal writings
- Any "treasures" you find outside, on your way to school or anywhere else
- Spelling lists
- Special notes or letters to or from you
- Special "pet" rock (may be painted in art class)
- Any medals or awards you earn this year (such as for track and field events)
- Notes to you from your teacher
- Any photographs you can spare
- Any object that will fit in your maleta, but not take up all the space

---

Quick Check: My Maleta, My Box of Memories

- Do I occasionally revisit the maletas when students are in small groups to carry out quick checks on the contents?

Steps for Students

1. Students bring small boxes with lids from home, or receive them from the teacher. They decorate their boxes in any creative way they want. They may glue bits and pieces, paint, color, whatever. It is important that their names show clearly on their maletas.
2. Students start saving things to put into their maletas. Checking the poster that the teacher has put up will let them see what sorts of things they can put in their boxes. If they are unsure about something, they should ask the teacher.
3. Students determine who they want to give their filled maletas to, and for what reason. (They may decide to keep them for themselves, and that's OK too.) In the meantime, even partially full maletas make good displays at interview or Open House times.
4. When their maletas are full, students give them away or save them in a special place.

Dealing with Diversities

Cultural: Encourage these children to discuss with others possible unusual items they might like to put in their boxes based on their cultural backgrounds. Celebrate the differences—this is a good opportunity to learn about other cultures.

Linguistic: Since the word "maleta" is Spanish, you have a wonderful opportunity to celebrate other languages. Invite children who speak other languages to share their words for suitcase; you may want students to change the name to one in the first language or to include more than one name on the boxes.

Religious: Some religions do not believe in the giving or receiving of gifts. If you have students from these backgrounds, be sure to check with parents before beginning this project. The students can still fill maletas, but the final purpose may be altered.

Socio-economic: These children may be upset by the prospect of having to come to school with a shoebox in good condition. Encourage them to ask at a local shoestore. If they are unsuccessful, assure them, in secret, that you can provide boxes.

Gifted: Challenge them to think of something special for the recipient of the filled maleta, such as a poem or drawing that reflects the interests of that person. For instance, if the intended recipient enjoys fly fishing, a student could research it and put in a report on that topic.

Dealing with Developmental Levels

Kindergarten to Grade 3: The only caution is to avoid letting children put absolutely *everything* in their boxes. They get so excited about this project that sometimes their maletas are bursting.

Grades 4 to 9: Encourage a good variety of writings and items in the boxes. Suggest doing some work just for the purpose of putting it in the boxes.

Making Curriculum Connections and More

Language Arts: Extensions include writing news articles for the school newsletter explaining the maleta and its purposes; writing friendly letters to accompany the giving of the maletas; listing other ways to convey the idea, such as "memory box" or "keepsake box"; and keeping a running record of maleta contents. Students could make charts or graphic organizers comparing maletas with other forms of remembering such as photographs and keepsakes. They could also identify possible applications and uses for the filled maletas through brainstorming, likely coming up with such ideas as writing stories about discovering the maletas fifty years in the future; writing poems about the maletas; sending the maletas to relatives who live far away; sharing the maletas with younger students, neighbors, or seniors; or arranging a display of many maletas for an Open House. Students could then choose one of these discussed uses and follow it through.

Health: Students could take an opportunity to discuss ways to show respect and appreciation of others; they could also compare the needs of adults and children—why might they give a filled maleta to an adult?

Social Studies: "My Maleta, My Box of Memories" could lead into researching how other people in history have "saved" memories. Students could also research explorers who may have left behind caches of objects to mark where they journeyed.

Lid-scape Landscapes

Like a fair house, built on another man's grave ...

What This Project Addresses

- problem solving, creativity, and generation of ideas
- group cooperation, cohesion, and responsibility
- information seeking; appreciation of the experience of others
- manual dexterity and hand-eye coordination
- patience and persistence
- curriculum connections: Language Arts, Health, Social Studies, Science, Mathematics, Art

Project Overview

Remember our fascination with model trains and the accompanying miniature towns and villages created specifically for the railway line to run through? "Lid-scape Landscapes" is a similar activity, minus the trains, and I've yet to find a student who didn't absolutely delight in the task.

Although this project may seem somewhat like "Heritage Home Display," which appears earlier in this chapter, it is really quite different. Beginning with a landscape, either from a Social Studies unit, a story shared in class, a novel study, or even from the imaginations of the students, the students create this vision in the lid of a box, using whatever materials they can find. The sides of the lid add stability and give something for materials to lean against or be attached to.

Here are a few landscapes that seem to work well with students:

- northern scenes (ice floes, icebergs, igloos, barren terrain ...)
- desert scenes (cacti, sand dunes, mud huts ...)
- mountain scenes (rocks, rivers, waterfalls, sparse trees, campsites, log cabins ...)
- meadow scenes (flowers, grasses, trees, animals, small rocks ...)
- ocean scenes (palm trees, water, gulls, sand, rocks, grass huts ...)
- fantasy scenes, such as Shakespeare's *Midsummer Night's Dream* seen through the eyes of children.

Wild and wonderful fantasy scenes make great *second* Lid-scapes to be done after a more limiting first one or after a great fantasy story shared in class.

But, of course, there are steps. This project involves much Synthesis on the part of the students, who first brainstorm their ideas, then illustrate them on paper, then collect materials, and finally, build their Lid-scapes. **Steps for Students** details how they will go about creating their masterpieces. Once they get started, it's usually difficult to keep them away from their evolving works of art. Be prepared to set time limits!

At the end of the year the Grade 3 teacher often received a plethora of notes, little gifts and such from "graduating" students, but one year, one note stood out. The carefully crafted letter came from a Métis boy who had had a difficult time adjusting to the school (he had arrived in October) and an even more difficult time with any literacy activities.

The teacher introduced "Lid-scape Landscapes" in February as a culminating activity to a class novel study, the setting of which had been the Canadian North. Although most of the groups decided to create snowy, northern landscapes, a few groups chose other settings, since the protagonist had lived first in Saskatchewan and then in Vancouver before moving north. Joe's group chose a Saskatchewan scene, and Joe just seemed to "come alive" with this project. Not only did he do the sketching for his group, it appeared he had most of the ideas too. When the Lid-scapes were all finished and on display, the teacher noticed that every morning Joe would check his group's project and make any necessary readjustments to the farming community they had built.

So when the letter arrived from Joe at the end of the year, the teacher was not surprised with its contents, although she was surprised at how well the note was written. This is what it said (reproduced exactly as it was received):

> Dear techer,
> This was the best school year ever. You made me do good on all my reading and writing becuse of the lidscaps. That was the best thing I ever did and it was fun to. I wish I could fail this year and stay here and make another lidscap again. Thank you very much for letting me do that thing. You made shule fun for me and I even got to like to write about the ldscap to. You are a good techer. Have a good life.
>
> Yurs truly, Joe

For building materials, refer to the list given for "Heritage Home Display" above.

Materials

- sturdy lids with sides, like the ones that come with paper stack boxes
- garbage bags for lining lids and cleaning up
- squares of felt
- white glue, scissors
- any building materials that you or the students can collect
- rocks of various sizes
- any miniature trees, bridges, and vehicles left over from young children's farm sets
- clay, putty, or Plasticine for "standing trees up in"
- roll of cotton batten (if making winter scenes)
- any solid color wrapping-paper scraps (shiny blue paper makes great lakes)
- dried grasses, sticks, Spanish moss and the like, available from craft stores

To introduce this project, ask, "If you could be anywhere in the world right now, where would it be?" Encourage discussion about different, interesting places students have heard or read about, or visited. Then explain that students are going to create some wonderful miniature places right in your classroom.

Steps for Teachers

1. Collect enough lids to provide at least one per group of four or five students. (Consider that "mistakes" may make extra lids necessary.)

2. Discuss landscapes with students. Share a few pictures or overheads or posters of different landscapes. If you want to limit students to landscapes related to a specific theme or topic, use these kinds of landscapes as prompts.
3. Break students into flexible, heterogeneous groups.
4. Once students understand the project and are working in groups, there will be little for you to do other than circulate and supervise. (Yeah!)

Quick Check: Lid-scape Landscapes

- Are the lids strong enough to support the settings? (Sometimes their integrity has been compromised and they may not stand up to what is in store for them.)
- Do I have enough "extra" supplies for groups that find themselves short?
- Do I have shelves prepared to store the works-in-progress as well as a large tabletop available to display the completed Lid-scapes?

Steps for Students

1. Once in their groups, students brainstorm about the kind of landscape they want to create and what sorts of things they will need to create it.
2. One member of each group draws what they want the finished Lid-scape to look like. The artist should make it an "overhead" view so that the group can use it as a sort of "map" when they begin building.
3. Students brainstorm for a list of materials they will need. One member writes the list and then it is divided among members who will locate the supplies. They start collecting supplies and keep them all in the lid until it is time to begin building.
4. When they begin building, students make the "ground" first. Will the bottom of the lid be covered with sand? green fabric? white cotton for snow? The groups work carefully and create a complete environment in their lids. They add as many details—miniature characters, houses, and more—as possible.
5. Students fasten each piece securely to the bottom, experimenting with putty, clay, and glue to find out what works best. If they have covered the lid with cotton batten, for instance, they may have to cut through it and fasten items directly to the cardboard lid.
6. When the Lid-scapes are finished, students give them names.

Dealing with Diversities

Cultural: Students from another country may be able to advise their groups on how to recreate interesting landscapes from their home countries, as long as you encourage this sort of diversity. If you and your students see this as an opportunity to learn more about the countries from which any *new* students have come, it can be a wonderful experience for all.

Linguistic: As long as the ESL students understand the project, they will contribute completely and in so doing, learn important language skills. A good idea is to have them keep a personal dictionary of the new words they learn associated with this project (e.g., *landscape, environment, habitat*).

Physical: If these students are unable to help build or create the Lid-scapes, suggest that they be the overseers who make recommendations.

Gifted: Challenge these students to write accurate descriptions of the Lid-scapes for the school newsletter or bulletins, or even to send to a local newspaper.

Dealing with Developmental Levels

Kindergarten to Grade 3: Very young children will need more help, but usually have more "items," such as small, plastic animals, houses, and cars, they can bring from home to add to the Lid-scapes. Their enjoyment of the project is not lessened by the fact that they are less able to create masterpieces.

Grades 4 to 9: I encourage you to let these students to try the fantasy genre of Lid-scape, as they excel here. I have also seen some amazing science-fiction creations complete with horrific aliens.

Making Curriculum Connections and More

Language Arts: Creative options include writing descriptions of the completed Lid-scapes, together with stories associated with them, which is especially fun when the Lid-scapes are fantasy based; placing familiar characters, such as themselves or peers, *in* their Lid-scapes and writing about what happens; and creating advertisements to encourage people to live in the environments created. Students could also experiment with words and sentence patterns to create word pictures describing their Lid-scapes for letters to go home or create word walls or personal word lists based on what was learned during this project.

Health: The class could discuss how people in different environments meet their basic needs. Students could also learn about family life in different cultures as suggested by the environments created.

Social Studies: Students could extend their study by examining and learning about historical landscapes, learning about real landforms and climates, or drawing maps of their Lid-scapes and then studying maps for topographical features.

Science: Research opportunities include finding out about the effects of climate and geographical features on life and ecosystems and the effects of global warming, pollution, and destruction of rain forests on all living things.

Mathematics: Students are obliged to consider weight and balance issues when working in the lids. They also have to measure accurately when building and record measurements.

Art: Extensions include making murals of the Lid-scapes as well as making posters to advertise the communities living in the Lid-scapes.

Fantasy Sandcastles

To sleep, perchance to dream—of castles in the air ...

What This Project Addresses

- communication and participation
- problem solving
- curiosity and inventiveness
- reflection and interpretation
- curriculum connections: Language Arts, Social Studies, Science, Mathematics, Art

Project Overview

Think summer! Think playing in the sun and sand. Now think of capitalizing on those wonderful feelings right here and now in your classroom! It's possible!

Before you scoff at the idea of any students over the age of six making sandcastles in school time, please read the rest of the information, and trust me when I say that even with Grade 9 students—yes, those big, almost-adult, rebellious Grade 9 students—this was an amazing project that not only got everyone involved, but was ranked number one on a "great things we did this year" survey.

Basically, this is a sandcastle building task, and it truly doesn't have to be messy! By using the right kinds of bases and limiting the amount of sand for each group, you remain in full control at all times. You simply challenge the students to build the most spectacular sandcastles they can, using only sand and water. At first they won't believe that this is not some sort of trick. Assure them it isn't and be prepared for some highly creative work.

TINY TRUE TALE

The following are words from a postcard received four years after a Grade 9 student took part in building sandcastles in class.

> Dear Ms. P,
> Here I am at a sandcastle building competition in Parksville, B.C. My team is awesome and we are going to win and then go to some place in the US where there is another competition. This is so cool. I just wanted to thank you for turning me on to sandcastle building in school.
> Yours truly,

Although I was pleased to hear from my former student, I would rather have turned him on to more than sandcastles. Still, every little bit counts!

Materials

- bases for the castles, one per group (first option best for washing, retaining dampness, and moving):
  1. Lids from big, plastic tote-storage containers
  2. Lids from aluminium garbage cans, *temporarily* flattened with a hammer, so that the lids lie flat

Encourage students to bring their own supply of sculpting materials from home. You will find that they are highly creative.

Introduce the project by asking students when any of them last built a sandcastle. Lead the discussion to the complexities and frustrations of sandcastle building—the incoming tide, the weight of the sand, the dog that runs through the castle, and so on. Then explain the project, and watch the surprised looks on their faces.

One of my biggest regrets was not having a camera when my Grade 9 students were up to their elbows in sand and smiling!

3. Cardboard lids from boxes of photocopy paper, lined with plastic bags
- sand, a "ten pound" bag per group, such as can be purchased for winter driving or at big home renovation stores
- water sprayers to keep the sand damp while working, one per group
- a container of water to initially damp the sand
- sculpting materials, ranging from spoons to pieces of flat wood

Steps for Teachers

1. Begin by introducing the topic of castles. What are they? Where are they? Then move to the idea of sandcastles. Be sure to show visuals of castles.
2. Discuss the various professional sandcastle building competitions that have become so popular of late—the one at Parksville, on Vancouver Island, is huge. If possible, locate pictures of some of these creations on the Internet and discuss how the builders might have managed these amazing feats.
3. Challenge the students, in groups, to come up with the most innovative sandcastle idea ever and to develop a group sketch.
4. Let them go to work, building their dream castles upon the bases chosen.

Quick Check: Fantasy Sandcastles

- Do I have a broom, mop, and dust pan ready for emergencies?
- Does each group have at least a couple of sculpting devices? (Have a few of your own ready just in case.)
- Do I have a camera ready to take those great shots of students playing in sand?

Steps for Students

1. In their groups, students design the most amazing sandcastle they can think of and have one member sketch it out.
2. They begin building by dampening some of their sand and making a mound in the base. Gradually, they add to the castle, spraying regularly with water to keep the sand damp and patting the sand firmly so that it maintains its shape.
3. Students add interesting features to their castles, such as small stones, sticks, feathers, and shells.
4. Each group comes up with a name for its castle.

Dealing with Diversities

Cultural: If you have students from another country, you may want to ask them if sandcastle building is popular there, and if so, would they like to share anything about it.

Behavioral and Motivational: Don't worry about them with this project. These students will *want* to cooperate.

Gifted: You may want these students to research sandcastle building *before* the project gets under way, and have them present their findings to the class. Similarly, challenge these students to research castles in general. They can follow this by doing in-depth research on one castle that interests them. (Always keep in mind the "instead-of" rule noted in the Introduction.)

Dealing with Developmental Levels

Kindergarten to Grade 3: Since they are masters at sandcastle building, all you may have to do is ration water and watch for "too mucky" sand. Invite them to bring sandcastle building "stuff" from home; many will have pails, shovels, and so on. To avoid the frustration of castles not living up to expectations, encourage them to build more common "at-the-beach" types of castles.

Grades 4 to 9: Challenge them to be very creative. Avoid the idea of competition between groups (although this will likely occur anyway) and celebrate all ideas. Once students buy into this project I think you'll be pleasantly surprised at the way they work together and accomplish interesting innovations on the basic sandcastle.

Making Curriculum Connections and More

Language Arts: Beyond recording the sequence of how the group went about building the castle, students could write stories about the inhabitants of the completed castles or descriptions of the interiors of the castles. Other options include creating charts, such as T-charts or innovative graphic organizers, to compare different completed castles.

Social Studies: Opportunities include researching the history and uses of castles, connecting ideas learned about castles to modern-day uses (many are museums or used for archives), and researching the daily life of people who lived at the time castles were built, while the castles were still in active use, or in castles in the modern world.

Science: Sandcastle building can lead into making predictions and generalizations (about the strength and standing capabilities of the castles) based on observations, describing the interaction of water with sand and applying that knowledge to practical problems of drying, and estimating effects of weight and pressure (on different parts of the sandcastles, for instance).

Mathematics: Students could go on to measure distances, shapes, and angles, and compare weights of dry and wet sand.

Art: When looking at art history, students could examine different types of castles and compare artistic styles. They might also imagine and draw various castle rooms, or create overhead maps indicating special features, such as hidden doors and tunnels.

Questions About Castles: A great extension of learning for this project is to ask the students what they can learn from the experience. Invite them to pose questions and then seek answers. Questions that students have asked include these:

- Why do some European castles seem to stand the test of time, while others built around the same time have crumbled?
- Why does another group's castle stand firmly while ours is falling?
- What are the ratios of water to sand that make sculpting easiest?
- Is there a way to preserve sandcastles forever (or at least for a long time)?
- Where are sandcastle building contests held?

Spectacular School Brochures

Sweet mercy is nobility's true badge.

What This Project Addresses

- school pride
- data compilation into meaningful presentations
- visual model construction—pictorial expression
- creativity and ingenuity
- communication
- curriculum connections: Language Arts, Health, Social Studies

Project Overview

Can you remember attending a school that you thought was just about the best ever? I hope so. I know I can. And I know that, as teachers, we want our students to feel that way about the schools in which we teach, because if they believe in their school, their overall performances will be better.

Travel brochures that illustrate exciting places and stimulating activities fascinate us all. Why not, then, create wonderful, amazing brochures about the place where we, and our students, spend the most time—the school? This project enables students to do just that.

After discussions and surveys to determine exactly what is great about the school—from the physical location and layout to the specific activities, teams, field trips, and even the staff—the students compile the information and create folded, information-filled bulletins that are colorful and inviting. They do this in pairs, folding an 8 by 11 page into three sections. (See Figure 26.)

The best part is that the brochures are authentic as they can be given to incoming students or community members, or even students from neighboring schools. In addition, the students' eyes are opened to the many merits of their school, some of which they may have been totally unaware. They gain a sense of pride and ownership, important for good school performance.

TINY TRUE TALE

Conversation overheard when students were working on their Spectacular School flyers:

"I didn't know there was so much good stuff in our school."
"Me neither. Boy, are we ever lucky, hey?"
"I guess. I still don't like school much."
"But what if you had to go to ___ School? That school doesn't have near as much good stuff as our school does."
"I guess. But I still don't like school."

Teacher's thoughts: Can't win them all …

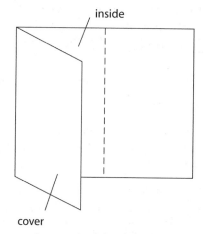

inside

cover

Spectacular School Brochure

Figure 26

Materials

- travel brochures as samples
- plain white paper

- an assortment of coloring materials, glue, and scissors
- magazines for cutting up
- computer word-processing program, if possible

Steps for Teachers

1. Prepare a list of the school's positive characteristics ahead of time. The list will help when it comes to brainstorming (and you won't forget something important like your amazing school secretary).
2. Begin by sharing and discussing travel brochures. *What makes them effective? Which ones are best? Why?*
3. Brainstorm all the positives of your school. You may want to list these on chart paper for future reference when students are "creating" their flyers.
4. If you are comfortable with it, allow students to "wander" the school, pens and paper in hands, to jot down good things they see. Give them a time limit for this: about fifteen minutes for Kindergarten to Grade 3 students; about a half-hour for older students.
5. Compare notes.

Quick Check: Spectacular School Brochures

- Are the pairs (chosen by me) working or do I need to make changes?
- Do I have a market for the finished flyers?
- Have I let the rest of the school know that my students will be doing "constructive wandering" on ___ at ___?

Steps for Students

1. Students find out as many good things about their school as possible. It's a good idea for them to consider it a game. They keep a list.
2. In partners, they plan their Spectacular School flyers. They fold a page into three equal parts, with the back of the left side becoming the front of the flyer.
3. They carefully design each section of the flyer, striving to be eye-catching, colorful, and neat. Each section should provide different information. It is important for them to remember that they are trying to *sell* the school. They can use anything they want to decorate the flyer to make it as amazing as their school. They may use the computer to make their printing perfect, but cannot use only that.

Dealing with Diversities

Cultural: Pair a new student with an "old" one. Doing this will provide an orientation for the new student (even though that will already have been done) and will highlight positive features that the student may have earlier missed.

Motivational and Behavioral: Invite these students to take charge of handing out the completed flyers, for example, taking a package of them to a nearby Kindergarten class or seniors' home. By involving them in this way, you may be able to offset any possible "I-don't-want-to" reactions.

Intellectual and Physical: You may wish to create a few groups of three to help these students.

Begin by sharing some travel brochures with the students and discussing the ways they appeal to us. Next, suggest that you have a challenge for them: to create similar brochures advertising their own school. Then launch a "Search and Seek" whereby the students brainstorm, collect information, and make charts of all the positives in their school. You'll be surprised at how many they come up with.

Gifted: Challenge these students to make use of figurative language and create similes, metaphors, and analogies for their flyers.

Dealing with Developmental Levels

I haven't found that any adaptations are necessary. The younger students simply make more basic flyers.

Making Curriculum Connections and More

Language Arts: Ideas include making lists, charts, and organizers of all the merits of the school, indicating which were "new" to the student; writing a news article about one positive aspect of the school; writing a letter to a group such as a seniors' home to ask permission to deliver flyers; or writing a letter to the editor of a local newspaper describing all the school's positive features.

Health: The original project helps develop pride in school; the class could take that further and discuss how to develop personal pride—how do we find out what's good about ourselves? Students could discuss the importance of acknowledging when people do "good things."

Social Studies: The class could build on the travel brochure idea by using maps to locate all the wonderful places talked about on travel brochures, researching and reporting to the class about any particular spot described in a travel brochure, or creating travel brochures for any country, civilization, or culture under study, such as the First Nations people.

Afterword

This is the short and the long of it.

Ask any students at the end of a school day what they did that day and more often than not the answer will be "nothin'." When a school year has ended, ask any students what they learned that year and it's probable that the answer will be a non-committal shrug of the shoulders. However, ask any one of them what specific thing they enjoyed most, and they will happily recall in vivid detail a project that fully engaged them. This is what education is all about—being engaged.

This emphasis is especially true when the classes are a wonderful mixture of children from different cultures, religions, ethnic backgrounds, first languages, and home environments, and every student exhibits varied degrees of ability and motivation. This is what today's classes are all about—variety.

A resource that enables busy teachers to reach all their students in authentic, purposeful, and relevant ways, and that still connects to the curriculum, is a valuable tool. This book of projects is intended to be just that. I hope you enjoy using it and that the suggestions offered within serve to make learning a little easier for everyone.

Appendix A: Understanding Cultural Diversity

Throughout my teaching career, my classrooms have included students from dozens of backgrounds and cultures. My work with teachers in training, many from an Aboriginal background, has taught me to better appreciate that students' cultural differences may be a factor in their classroom behavior. Frequently, student teachers, new teachers, or even seasoned teachers faced with a diversity of cultural backgrounds in their classes have asked for guidance in this matter. They want to be familiar with any cultural behaviors or nuances of behavior that might appear "different" from what they have come to expect in a classroom. Below I have identified some of the things that my students from a wide range of backgrounds and cultures have clarified for me. The ideas are generalizations—not all students will exhibit any particular behaviors in a given situation—so be sure to use this appendix as a guideline only. Always remember that students are unique and need to be treated as individuals first.

Eye Contact: (Asian, Aboriginal) Avoiding eye contact is polite and respectful. Although eye contact is deemed important for respectful conversation and attention in European cultures, it is rude in these cultures.

Cooperation: (Southeast Asian, Polynesian, Aboriginal) These children are taught to cooperate, to help one another, to avoid one-upmanship. Therefore they are not "competitive" and can feel threatened by competitive activities.

Tardiness: (Aboriginal) Time has an entirely different meaning to First Nations children; habitual tardiness should be examined through their eyes and a mutual understanding reached.

Risk Taking (learning through mistakes): (Japanese) Teachers typically encourage risk taking, but in some cultures, notably Japanese, correctness is valued more. In Japan, as well as some other Asian countries, students are taught not to guess or take risks. What may appear as refusal to cooperate, may be unwillingness to make a mistake.

"Show-off" Activities, such as Show and Tell (or being first in line ...): (Aboriginal, certain religious groups such as Mennonite and Hutterite) Any behavior that attracts attention to self is discouraged, so teachers must consider the cultural implications of activities that require the child to be other than modest.

Informal Classroom Environment: (European, Asian, Muslim) Canadian teachers are taught to be relatively informal in the classroom, whereas in some cultures school is much more formal. Students from these backgrounds often view our schools as chaotic and loud. They may interpret informality as permission to misbehave.

Responding to Questions/Taking Part in Discussions: (Aboriginal) In Aboriginal cultures, one does not offer advice unless explicitly asked for it. Consequently, these students may be reluctant to answer out in class unless a question is specifically directed to them. As a rule, silence is comfortable for them; this may be seen as insubordination if teachers are unaware of the cultural background for the behavior.

Possession of "Goods": (Hutterite, other religious groups, Aboriginal, to a certain extent) In some cultures or colonies goods are owned collectively; personal ownership and pride are discouraged. This may have an effect on certain in-class practices where, for instance, children are asked to bring items from home.

Time Needed to Respond: (Aboriginal) Patience is valued by this culture. Teachers may feel discouraged with the time that students (and parents) take to respond to questions or information. European cultures appear to "move too quickly" as far as Aboriginal children are concerned. Rather than being lazy, students may just be behaving in the slow, deliberate manner of their culture.

Social Distance: (Asian, certain religious sects, Muslim) In some cultures, children are taught to keep a social distance between students and teachers. These students are, therefore, uncomfortable with "grand discussions" or informal activities. They may view the more casual relationships between students and teachers, especially in the higher grades, as an invitation to misbehave.

Differing Parental Expectations: (Asian) In some cultures parents equate learning and knowledge with memorization of facts; lots of homework is expected and parents are upset if it is not forthcoming.

Differences in Child-Rearing Practices: (Aboriginal, Muslim) In some cultures, child rearing may be considered permissive by European standards. Teachers may mistakenly feel parents "do not care" or "are not interested" when the child does something inappropriate; instead, the parent(s) may be choosing to allow the child a measure of independence. It is also important to note that relatives in Aboriginal families often function exactly as parents. In other homes, there may be obvious differences in expectations for boys and girls. Teachers must be aware of where parents stand on this issue, especially if a brother and sister are in the same class.

Expression of Emotions: (Asian, Aboriginal, some religious groups) Although expression of emotion is generally encouraged in European culture, many cultures do the opposite. Students from these cultures may seem aloof or reserved, when, in fact, they are following their cultural heritage. It may make the student extremely uncomfortable if the teacher unwittingly insists on an expression of emotion.

Appendix B: When Alternative Activities Are Required

It is important to know if there are students in your class who, for religious reasons, are not allowed to take part in traditional activities such as making Christmas or Halloween crafts or even doing writing tasks based on these days. These students will require alternative authentic activities planned in advance.

Although there may be many diverse beliefs that affect students' participation, I offer a few that seem to crop up the most frequently in our schools.

> Groups that cannot participate in traditional activities pertaining to special days such as Halloween and Christmas, or any activities outside the boundaries of their religion, include the following:
>
> - Jehovah's Witnesses
> - Evangelical Christians (Halloween)
> - Hindu
> - Buddhist (no focus on material things; hence, no "gift exchange")
> - Sikh

Below is a list of alternatives to traditional holiday-related activities to ensure that some students are not simply doing "busy work" or, worse still, "sitting alone in the library":

- drawing, illustrating symbols of their religions, or symbols or items important to their specific cultures (rather than, for instance, doing Christmas projects)
- preparing presentations about ethnic or cultural celebrations (rather than reading holiday-related materials)
- researching ethnic or culture related topics
- being "big-buddy helpers" in other classes if the home class is involved in some holiday-related activity
- creating posters celebrating ethnic or cultural backgrounds while the rest of the class is creating holiday-related posters, cards, or decorations

Note: It is a good idea to invite all parents to your class early in the term for an informal evening forum to discuss ethnic, cultural, and religious ideas, concerns, and limitations, and brainstorm together for alternative activities in which they would like to see their children involved. In this way you will have an accurate account of "who can do what." This, coupled with a parent take-home questionnaire, will take the guesswork out of your plans and prevent any unnecessary headaches that can crop up simply because you "didn't know."

Appendix C: Good Ideas for Dealing Effectively with Aboriginal or Non-Dominant Culture Students

- Present Aboriginal or non-dominant culture students with appropriate role models and with authentic literary characters with whom students can identify.
- Look for books and other materials authentically written by their own people.
- Avoid any arts or crafts that trivialize the dress, dance, ceremonies or ways of any group or culture.
- Make sure you know the accurate history of people indigenous to your country or area, and endeavor to include this information as a part of dominant culture history study.
- Use books, reports, magazines, and other materials that accurately put Native history in perspective.
- Always present cultural heroes who fought to defend their own people, who demonstrate the positive aspects of the culture, and with whom the students will be able to identify.
- Discuss the relationship between Native peoples and colonists and what went wrong with it, showing both sides of the big picture.
- Use materials that show respect for, and understanding of, the sophistication and complexities of Native and other cultural societies.
- Use respectful language, and avoid tokenism by not "throwing in a word or two of another language when teaching about another culture."
- Use materials that show the continuity of Native societies, with traditional values and spiritual beliefs connected to the present.
- Portray Natives as the original inhabitants of our land.
- Invite Native or other culture elders or community members to class; be sure to treat them as teachers, not entertainers. Offer an honorarium, if feasible.
- Talk about the lives of Native peoples and people of any non-dominant cultures in the present.
- Whenever possible, read, discuss, and make readily available in your room good poetry suitable for kids by contemporary Native and other culture writers.
- Celebrate given and family names in as many ways as possible.
- If possible, plan at least one theme around the Native culture integrated in a cross-curricular manner, and one around other diverse cultures.
- Portray Native societies as coexisting with nature in a delicate balance, in a manner from which we can, and should, learn.
- Celebrate all languages by using primary source material in the forms of speeches, songs, poems, and writings. Try to show the linguistic skill of peoples who come from an oral tradition.
- Make a point of learning as much as possible about the cultures of all students in your class, keeping in mind that everyone originally comes from a culture other than the currently dominant one.
- Treat the Aboriginal children and children of various ethnic groups as exciting spokespersons for their culture or religion—see them as a valuable resource.
- Acknowledge orally and often the benefits of having Aboriginal children as well as children from a variety of backgrounds in your class.

- Discuss the connection between Aboriginal language and culture, roots, identity, social, spiritual, and emotional well-being, as well as the connections between any other languages spoken by students in your class.
- Consider in-class ways to revive Native or other first languages. Discuss this with the community if possible.
- Acknowledge diversity *within* Aboriginal groups and within other cultural, ethnic, or religious groups. *No two children are the same, regardless of where they were born or how they were raised.*
- Clarify what the word "traditional" means when used. Traditional today may not have been traditional in the days before European contact.
- Ensure that students see Aboriginal knowledge as inter-connected with many fields of thought (a "wholistic" point of view).
- Use a variety of assessment techniques so that you can fairly assess students no matter what diversities they present. Remember Howard Gardiner's concept of multiple intelligences.
- Adopt a multi-generational, rather than a short-term vision. Consider how what you are teaching will help future generations.

Appendix D: Multi-linguistic Crossword Puzzle

						M						
						U						
						T		m			B	
				m	o	T^t	h	e	r		R	
				a		E		r			U	
				i		R		e			D	
	H^h	o	u	s	e	V					E	
	A			o		f	A^a	t	h	e	R^r	
	U			n		T						
	S		é			p	E_e	r	e			
		s	t	a	r		R			f		
			o							r		
			i		b	r	o	t	h	e	r	
			l							r		
	S	T	E^e	R	N					e		

→ English (lower case)
⇩ French (lower case) ⎫ or color code
⇩ GERMAN (upper case) ⎭

* Limit to two languages if desired.

- mother
- father
- house
- star
- brother

Note: Not all accents are shown.

Appendix E: New Names

Chart 1

Use the *first* letter of your name to determine your new *first* name.

A = STINKY   J = POOPSIE   R = LOOPY
B = LUMPY   K = FLUNKY   S = SNOTTY
C = BUTTERCUP   L = BOOGER   T = FALAFEL
D = GIDGET   M = PINKY   U = DORKY
E = CRUSTY   N = ZIPPER   V = SQUEEZIT
F = GREASY   O = GOOBER   W = OPRAH
G = FLUFFY   P = DOOFUS   X = SKIPPER
H = CHEESEBALL   Q = SLIMY   Y = DINKY
                                         Z = ZSA ZSA

[For "I," take the second letter.]

Chart 2

Use the *first* letter of your *last* name to determine the *first* half of your new last name.

A = DIAPER   J = MONKEY   R = GIZZARD
B = TOILET   K = POTTY   S = PIZZA
C = GIGGLE   L = LIVER   T = GERBIL
D = BUBBLE   M = BANANA   U = CHICKEN
E = GIRDLE   N = RHINO   V = PICKLE
F = BARF   O = BURGER   W = CHUCKLE
G = LIZARD   P = HAMSTER   X = TOFU
H = WAFFLE   Q = TOAD   Y = GORILLA
                                         Z = STINKER

Chart 3

Use the *last* letter of your *last* name to determine the second half of your new last name.

A = HEAD   J = HONKER   R = BUNS
B = MOUTH   K = BUTT   S = FANNY
C = FACE   L = BRAIN   T = SNIFFER
D = NOSE   M = TUSHIE   U = SPRINKLES
E = TUSH   N = CHUNKS   V = KISSER
F = BREATH   O = HiNEY   W = SQUIRT
G = PANTS   P = BISQUITS   X = HUMPERDINK
H = SHORTS   Q = TOES   Y = BRAINS
I = LIPS   Z = JUICE

Source: *From CAPTAIN UNDERPANTS AND THE PERILOUS PLOT OF PROFESSOR POOPYPANTS by Dav Pilkey. Published by the Blue Sky Press/Scholastic Inc. Copyright ©2000 by Dav Pilkey. Reprinted by permission.*

Appendix F: Story Theatre—Red and the Wolf

Note: Each character says everything EXCEPT what is in parentheses.

Red: Once upon a time there was a sweet little girl, (*smiles*) who was very cute and adorable and well behaved and ...

Mother: Her mother, who was very kind and wise, interrupted the girl and said I have a chore for you.

Red: Red was happy. She loved to do chores for her dear mumsy because she was about the sweetest little ...

Mother: (*to audience*) Isn't she adorable? Then the mother said to Red, here, take this to Grannie, (*starts miming sweeping*) and then the overworked mother went back to her daily chores.

Red: Red skipped off happily to Gran's, but on the way

Wolf: she met a wolf—big, mean, but unusually handsome (*smiles at audience*). Now the wolf was cunning, so he tricked the girl into telling him where she was going. (*to Red*) So, it's off to Grannie's, hey?

Red: Red was a bit confused. She knew wolves were dangerous, but he looked so, well, adorable that she told him everything. (*shrugging to audience*) How could you blame her?

Wolf: (*miming running*) The wolf, being in excellent shape from good nutrition and daily exercise, beat the girl to Grannie's house.

Red: (*miming walking slowly, looking at sky, picking flowers*) And Red just took her time. She was in no hurry.

Grannie: Meanwhile, Grannie, wise old lady that she was, saw the wolf coming and made ready. She assumed her best self-defence pose and waited behind the door. (*She assumes a "Karate-kid" pose.*)

Wolf: When wolf entered ...

Grannie: (*doing the actions as she talks them*) Grannie jumped out and karate-chopped him in the head

Wolf: and the poor unsuspecting, trusting wolf, fell to the floor.

Red: When Red finally arrived, she saw Grannie standing over the poor defenceless wolf and was horrified. (*to Grannie, trying to restrain her*) Dear grandmother, what are you doing to this poor defenceless creature?

Wolf: Wolf was glad to see Red. (*to Red, from his position on the floor*) Hi Red, he said.

Red: Oh, hi wolf. (*to Grannie*) Now you stop this at once, elder person. Wolves are on the endangered list and ...

Woodcutter: (*entering with much drama*) and at that minute the tall, dark, and handsome woodcutter entered the premises. Looking shocked (*pauses to look shocked at both Red and then audience*), he said, What's going on here?

Red: Red Riding Hood took it upon herself to do the introductions. Oh hi, Woodcutter, she said. I'd like you to meet my gran (*Red points, Gran stops her fighting and shakes hands with Woodcutter*) and the wolf (*Wolf gets up, dusts himself off and salutes*)

Woodcutter: The woodcutter smiled and said, and who might you be, little lady?

Red: Oh, said Red, I'm the well-known sweet and lovely Red Riding Hood.

Grannie: Grannie was tired of being ignored so she said, well, if all this nonsense is over, I'm off to my ballet lessons. Lock up when you leave, dear. And with that the grandmother, who certainly didn't look her age, danced off into the night. (*She dances off.*)

Woodcutter: Leaving just the wolf, the girl and the woodcutter alone in the cottage. Well, said the woodcutter, what should we do with Mr. Wolf here?

Red: Red thought for a moment (*puts her finger to her cheek miming thinking*) then she said, I think we should just let him go as long as he promises not to bother my grannie again.

Wolf: (*kneeling*) The grateful wolf said, Oh thank you, Red. I promise.

Red: And so Little Red Riding Hood

Woodcutter: and the woodcutter

Wolf: and the big bad wolf who wasn't big and bad any more

Red: lived happily … (*linking her arm through the woodcutter's*)

Woodcutter: ever…

Wolf: after. The end!

Appendix G: Tune Time

These suggestions pertain to the project "Innovative Instruments." The questions and activities can serve as a starting point for further differentiated activities such as personal reflections or discussions.

Talking about the song or music:

- What do the words in the song mean?
- Are there any unusual words in the song? What do they mean? How do you know? How do you figure out what words mean?
- Are there any nonsense words used? If so, why do you think the composer has used them? Can you do this in prose or expository writing?
- What lyrics or words do you like or dislike? Why?
- Are some parts of the song or words repeated? Why do you think that is? Could you use this idea of repetition in prose writing?
- Do you see evidence of "poetic licence," or some place where the song writer has broken established rules for effect?
- Are some words shortened in non-standard ways? For example: "takin'" instead of "taking." Can you do this in narrative writing? (yes, in dialogue) In expository writing?
- Is symbolism used? If so, what is it, and why do you think it's there?
- Are there analogies or figures of speech? For example: "meaner than a junkyard dog." How could you use this idea in prose writing?
- Do you like or dislike the melody? How does the melody help or hinder the overall effect of the tune?

You can also use these ideas for personal reflections.

Writing about or illustrating the song or music:

- Illustrate the song. (You might make cartoons, posters, abstract paintings, or clay shapes.)
- Write a good sentence about the song.
- Write another verse for the song.
- Combine two songs into one. (It's fun to work with simple songs such as "Twinkle, Twinkle" and "Three Blind Mice.")
- Use a tune for learning about, reviewing, or reinforcing study of punctuation, spelling, word skills, sequencing, capitalization, or comprehension.
- On a "Tune Talk" bulletin board for the class, add names of favorite songs, brief explanations of why you like them and illustrations, if you wish. (Your teacher may encourage you to consider uncommon genres or periods by having special days for tunes from your "parents' time," tunes that are funny, or tunes from the Second World War.)
- Make the song into a picture book for a specific audience, such as senior citizens or Kindergarten students.
- Write a story, paragraph, or essay based on the music's moral, lesson, or thought, if applicable.
- Find another song with a similar meaning. Compare the two songs with a visual organizer, such as a T-chart or Venn diagram.

- Research the singer or composer; write an autobiography or research report.
- Select a tune you "wouldn't normally choose." Perhaps your choice will come from a different culture or time period. Analyze the music in detail for melody, lyrics and overall appeal.
- Make a tune anthology by collecting favorite songs, writing out the lyrics, illustrating them, and recording personal feelings about the songs.
- Use a tune to help promote higher level thinking skills, such as synthesizing, evaluating, or predicting.
- Look for both figurative and literal meanings in lyrics. Why do you think that songs often rely on figurative meaning?
- Do a survey of favorite songs. Solicit responses from a variety of people; then create graphs, charts or other visual organizers with the information gathered. The survey can be open-ended. *What is your favorite?* Or, it can be limited. *What is your favorite pop song? classical piece?*
- Examine tunes from a variety of cultures. How do they reflect the cultures?
- Find some songs that rhyme and some that do not. Which do you prefer and why?

Performing the song or music:

- "Sing" or act out the song with hand puppets or finger puppets.
- Mime what is happening in the song or what the music makes you think of.
- Create an air band using either home-made or "pretend" instruments.
- Keep the rhythm by clapping, stamping, or using rulers or rhythm band instruments.
- Create sequenced movements or a dance based on a familiar song.
- Take part in a full class singsong. The class could learn an unusual song, perhaps with accompaniment on a CD. Students might complement their singing with actions. **Note:** This can become a great concert presentation!

Appendix H: Culturally Divergent Books: A Recommended List

Picture Books—Narrative

Asha's Mums, by Rosamund Elwin, Michele Paulse, and Dawn Lee
A Small Tall Tale from the Far Far North, by Peter Sis
Boys Don't Knit, by Janice Schoop; illustrated by Laura Beingessner
Crabs for Dinner, by Adwoa Badoe
From Far Away, by Robert Munsch and Saoussan Askar; illustrated by Michael Martchenko
Knots on a Counting Rope, by Bill Martin Jr.; illustrated by John Archambault
Liang and the Magic Paintbrush, by Demi
Mei Mei Loves the Morning, by Margaret Holloway Tsubakiyama, Cornelius Van Wright, and Ying-Hwa Hu
Murdo's Story: A Legend from Northern Manitoba, as told by Murdo Scribe
Rose Blanche, by Roberto Innocenti
Selina and the Bear Paw Quilt, by Barbara Smucker; illustrated by Janet Wilson
Sitti's Secrets, by Naomi Shihab Nye; illustrated by Nancy Carpenter
Something from Nothing, by Phoebe Gilman
Subira Subira, by Tololwa M. Mollel; illustrated by Linda Saport
The Man Who Became an Eagle, a Haida legend retold by John Enrico
The Polar Bear Son: An Inuit Tale, by Lydia Dabcovich
The Rough-faced Girl, by Rafe Martin; illustrated by David Shawn
Two Pairs of Shoes, by Esther Sanderson
You Are Special, by Max Lucado; illustrated by Sergio Martinez

Picture Books—Informational

Look to the North: A Wolf Pup Diary, by Jean Craighead George; illustrated by Lucia Washburn
Make Your Own Inuksuk, by Mary Wallace

Picture Book—Poetry

If You Could Wear My Sneakers, by Sheree Fitch; illustrated by Darcia Labrosse

Professional Resources

Celebrating Our Cultures: Language Arts Activities for Classroom Teachers, by Barbara Dumoulin and Sylvia Sikundar
Windows on the World: Plays and Activities Adapted from Folk Tales from Different Lands, by Sylvia Sikundar and Diane Williams

Chapter Books

Mud City, by Deborah Ellis
The Tale of a Silly Goose & Other Stories, by Vicki Rogers and Sharon Stewart
Walk Two Moons, by Sharon Creech (A Newbery Medal Book)

Index